HUNTING IN THE HIMALAYA

HUNTING IN THE HIMALAYA

R. H. W. DUNLOP

GYAN

Published by

Gyan Publishing House
5, Ansari Road
Daryaganj, New Delhi-110002
Phone: 011-47034999, 9811692060
E-mail: books@gyanbooks.com

Distribution Network
gyanbooks.com
India, USA, Canada, UK, Australia

ISBN: 978-93-7225-638-3 (HB)

First Published, 1860

2nd Impression 2026

Printed at: Gyan Press, Delhi.

HUNTING IN THE HIMALAYA
Author: R. H. W. DUNLOP

J. Wolf del.

J. & J. Hanhart, Lith.

HUNTING

IN

THE HIMALAYA.

WITH

NOTICES OF CUSTOMS AND COUNTRIES
FROM THE ELEPHANT HAUNTS OF THE DEHRA DOON,
TO THE BUNCHOWR TRACKS IN ETERNAL SNOW,

BY R. H. W. DUNLOP, C.B. B.C.S. F.R.G.S.

AUTHOR OF "ADVENTURE WITH THE KHAKEE RESSALAH."

ILLUSTRATED BY J. WOLF.

LONDON:
RICHARD BENTLEY, NEW BURLINGTON STREET.
1860.

TO

F. S. WIGRAM, ESQ. B.C.S.

THE TYPE OF WHAT A SPORTSMAN SHOULD BE,

AND BUT LATELY MY COMPANION, THROUGH OTHER HUNTING GROUNDS,

WHERE, SPORT AND SKIRMISH, DEER-SHOOTING AND STERNER DUTIES ALTERNATED,

I DEDICATE, (NOW SEVEN THOUSAND MILES AWAY), THESE DETAILS OF

HIMALAYAN EXPERIENCES.

CONTENTS.

CHAPTER I.

INTRODUCTORY.

CHAPTER II.

ELEPHANT HUNTING.

CHAPTER III.

ELEPHANT HUNTING.

CHAPTER IV.

TIGER SHOOTING.

CHAPTER V.

GENERAL DOON SHOOTING.

CHAPTER IX.

IN THE SNOW RANGES.

CHAPTER X.

BEYOND THE SNOWS.

CHAPTER XI.

IN THIBET.

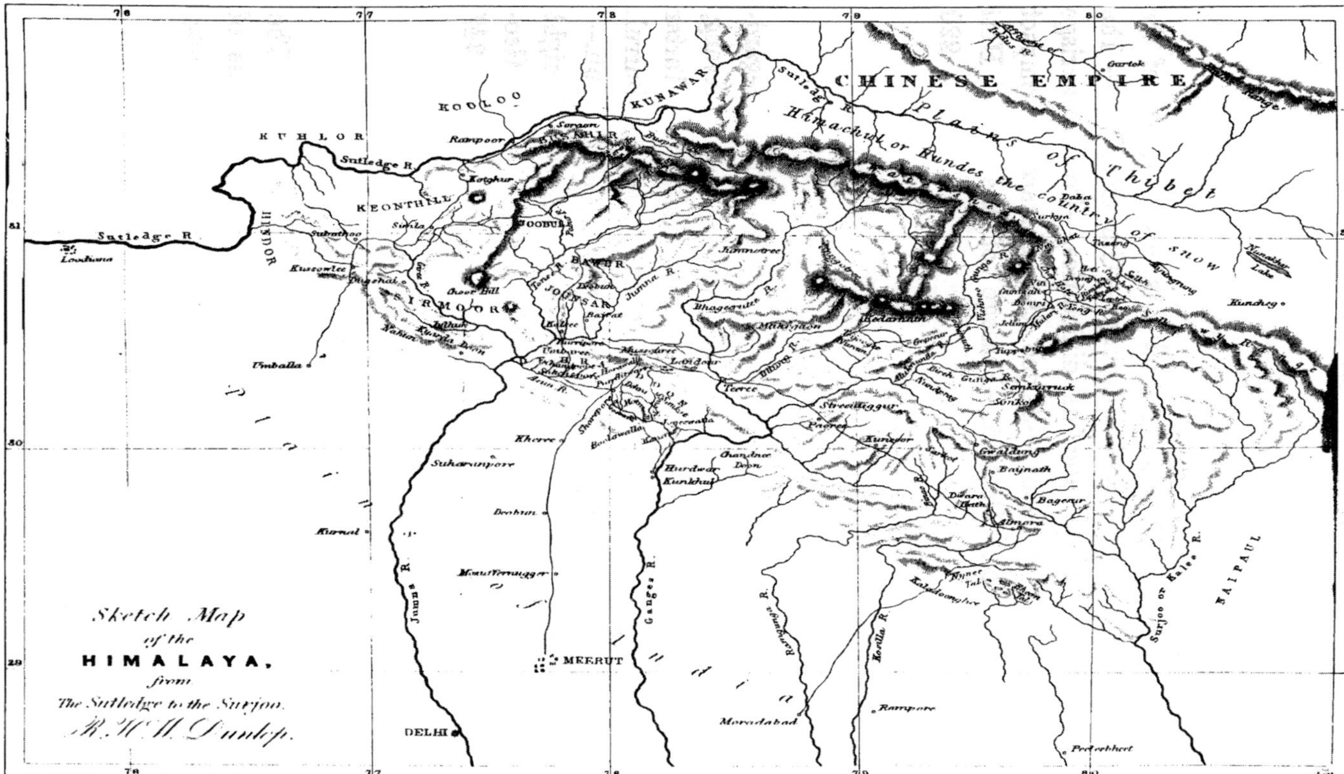
Sketch Map
of the
HIMALAYA,
from
The Sutledge to the Surjoo.
R. H. W. Dunlop.
CHINESE EMPIRE
Plains of Thibet
Himachul or Hundes the country of snow
KUHLOR
KOOLOO
KUNAWAR
KEONTHILL
HINDOR
SIRMOOR
JOUNSAR
BAWUR
JOOBUL
BAIPAUL
Sutledge R.
Jumna R.
Ganges R.
Bhageerutee R.
Ramgunga R.
Kosilla R.
Surjoo or Kalee R.
Indus R.
Loodiana
Umballa
Kurnal
Suharunpore
Deobun
Mozuffernuggur
MEERUT
DELHI
Moradabad
Rampore
Pileebheet
Rampoor
Kotghur
Simla
Subathoo
Kussowlee
Choor Hill
Hurdwar
Kunkhul
Kheree
Chandnee Doon
Kedarnath
Mukhaon
Streenuggur
Terree
Landour
Mussooree
Kuneedor
Gwaldum
Baijnath
Bageswur
Almora
Sonkot
Nynee Tal
Gartok
Daba
Kunchog
Lake
London Richard Bentley 1860

HUNTING

IN

THE HIMALAYA.

CHAPTER I.

INTRODUCTORY.

Plan of Campaign.—Parallels and approaches.—Sketch of the Ground.—Proper Seasons for Hunting in the several localities.—List of articles to be taken from England.—List of articles to be got in India.—Expense of camp life in the Hills, and cost of trip out.—Lists and local names of the game, &c., to be met with in the Doon.—Lists and local names of the game, &c., to be met with in the Hills.—Lists and local names of the game, &c., to be met with beyond the Snows.

SEEING, since my return to England, how many spend time, trouble, and money on deer-stalking and bird-shooting in Scotland, I conclude that it must arise chiefly from non-acquaintance with the facilities for reaching the Himalaya, and obtaining an almost endless assortment of game there, that our English sportsmen do not, if only for the sake of variety, attempt enterprizes more worthy of their energies.

It has been said, that hunting instincts more or less pervade all nature, but Anglo-Saxons are the only true sportsmen in the world; and, in the case of English gentlemen, there is no doubt but that instinct and habit, alternately cause and effect, do much in producing that activity, and energy of mind and body, that promptitude in danger, and passion for fair play, which they carry with them wherever they wander.

Never having passed a hot season in the plains without being prostrated by fever, and devoting invariably any sick leave I could obtain during convalescence to travelling in the Hills, my wanderings there have been frequent.

I have no intention of attempting any

journalistic account of my various expeditions through Kumaon, Gurhwal, and Sirmour, Kooloo, Kanawur, and Tartary, but will give my march in the last, as the tract least known, somewhat in detail, and trace most of my tours on the sketch map accompanying this volume.

I digress without reserve into topics incidental to hill travel, though not properly to hunting, on the ground that "Perdrix, toujours perdrix," may surfeit even a lover of game; and the details I give, being the result of practical experience, may, I hope, afford some information on an interesting locality insufficiently known.

I would rather succeed in the matter than the manner of my book, and trust I may be excused for quoting the following passage from Lewes' Life of Goethe, as being somewhat illustrative. "A Frenchman, an Englishman, and a German were commissioned to give the world the benefit of their views on that interesting animal, the camel. Away goes the Frenchman to the *Jardin des Plantes*, spends an hour there in rapid investigation, returns, and writes a *feuilleton,* in which there is no phrase which the Academy can blame, but also no phrase which adds to the general knowledge. He is perfectly satisfied however, and says, *Le voilà, le Chameau !*

"The Englishman packs up his tea-caddy, and a magazine of comforts; pitches his tent in the East; remains there studying the camel in its habits; and returns with a thick volume of facts, arranged without order, expounded without philosophy, but serving as valuable materials for all who come after him. The German despising the frivolity of the Frenchman, and the unphilosophical matter of factness of the Englishman, retires to his study, there *to construct the idea of a camel from out of the depths of his moral consciousness.*"

If this record is found to contain the good leaven of our national peculiarity, so quaintly described in this quotation, I shall feel content though convicted also of its defects.

The game of India, like much else which we deem characteristic of, and therefore common in that country, does not necessarily become familiar to mere length of residence; many persons, ladies especially, may live twenty or thirty years in India, without ever seeing a live snake, except in the hands of a native juggler or snake charmer, though some of their sisters at home believe them to be as common as spiders and black-beetles here, and capable of visiting bed-rooms, and sleeping under pillow cases with alarming familiarity. There are some old women of both sexes who pass a life-time in the country, without ever having seen any of our larger game, or knowing more of their habits and habitat than their friends at home, whose imagination, assisted by the letters of powerful correspondence commissioners, may picture a perfect menagerie scared off a railway by the whistle of a steam engine, while snakes and monkeys festoon the telegraph wires. Have you ever killed a tiger? is a question sometimes put to Anglo-Indians, who are just as likely to have killed a sea-serpent.

Hunting in the Himalaya, at least, cannot be purchased all made easy for money as in

Britain, or the birds found for you with all the comfort and certainty of pheasants at a battue, or poultry in Covent Garden market; but the exercise of the judgment, the sharpening of the faculties, and the keen discrimination requisite for success, constitute the chief charm of Himalayan hunting to the true sportsman, and, I believe, the surest attraction for the majority of that class who visit our highland moors and deer forests.

Although, however, a certain amount of labour is necessary in acquiring the minutiæ of local knowledge necessary for success at any spot chosen as a hunting site, yet a great amount of general experience may be obtained from practical records of sporting adventure. I have often longed, when I commenced my career, for some book that would give me details of information on points which I have had to determine for myself, at a great waste of time and trouble.

I am desirous, therefore, of making my experience practically useful to all who may be willing to take a six weeks' voyage for the sake of Indian hunting, or for those whose destiny sends them on duty or sick leave to the Himalaya.

There is a great similiarity in the kinds of game to be met with at the same altitudes throughout the entire length of the hills; *i. e.*, from Cashmere to Cachar. The only difference in birds is in the case of the loongee, or argus pheasant, one species only being found in Kumaon, another in Gurhwal, and a third in Kangra; as a general rule, too, the burrul, or wild snow sheep of the Kumaon and Gurhwal snows, gives place to the skene, or ibex, west of the Sutledge, which again gives place to the markhor, or spiral-horned wild goat, and the hangul, or twelve-tined stag of Cashmere. I purpose then in order to familiarise the reader with the different kinds of Himalayan game, to take a cross section of the Hills, beginning with the slopes at the foot of them in the valley of the Dehra Doon, and passing in review the game of the several ranges to the table lands of Thibet, beyond the Eternal Snows. Such a cross section embraces one hundred miles of territory in a direct line, but numberless deep descents and ascents, long circuits, and an immense amount of exercise to the pedestrian hunter, which, however, the gloriously inspirating air of those snowy altitudes, enables him thoroughly to enjoy.

I have given at the end of this chapter a list of the articles with which a sportsman bent on a tour to the Himalayas should supply himself; and we will now suppose him to have taken his passage out to Calcutta overland, or by the Great Eastern, and run up from the City of Palaces through the dead levels of Bengal and the north-western provinces by E. I. Railway to Meerut; this line is not yet completed, but soon will be. The traveller will pass numberless dreary and desolate looking stations en route, where the late Company's, now Her Majesty's, servants, civil and military, are on duty, in places less cheerful than English Penitentiaries, and a climate which during the hot weather and rains, or eight months of the year, is, "I guess," more diabolical than purgatory.

The four cold months are November, December, January, and February, and visitors should time their arrivals during one of these, when even the plains stations begin to look comparatively cheerful, and the European inhabitants healthy and happy.

From Meerut to the Valley of the Doon, a distance of about one hundred miles, some little experience in dawk travelling (Indian posting) will be acquired.

The higher ranges of the Himalaya are visible from Meerut during the rains, but at other seasons they are not seen till the traveller enters the district of Saharanpore, and when from fifty to one hundred miles from the foot of them, the distance depending on the state of the atmosphere. The Sewalik Hills which bound the Doon to the south, and are therefore some twenty miles nearer, soon after appear, they are of comparatively insignificant height, from five to six hundred feet, but make as a foreground, with the giant hills behind them, a scene scarce equalled elsewhere.

Throughout the journey from Calcutta, and at Meerut, Dehra, and Mussouree, there are hotels which, though not on the scale of European inns, are well suited to the requirements of the country, and as comfortable as any sportsman will desire. Beyond Mussouree in the hills, and even while hunting in the Doon he must be as independant almost as a gipsey; but in exchange for the comforts of houses and town life, to say nothing of the sport for which he has come, he can roam at will over lands unfettered by hedges, dikes, and ditches, and destitute of all warning notices as to steel traps, spring guns, and prosecutions with the utmost rigour of the law.

The valley of the Dehra Doon is bounded by the Himalaya to the north, the Sewalik to the south, and the rivers Ganges and Jumna to the east and west. It is about forty miles in extreme length and sixteen across. The Sewalik Hills extend beyond its southern boundary both to the east and westward, they are about eight to ten miles across, and are a mass of boulder and sandstone hills broken up into fantastic shapes by innumerable ravines, which are, generally speaking, quite dry, except on the southern extremity, where a thin thread of water remains perennially in each, and a plentiful supply of very small fish, called chilwas, are got from them. In the rainy season, sudden floods, or "raos" in the vernacular, sweep through, carrying away all that opposes them, and sometimes endangering travellers or property passing at that season, the roads or ghât routes through the range being generally along some of these torrent beds. Captain Burton in his "Pilgrimage to El-Medinah and Mecca" adopts the word "iumara," as exactly expressing the kind of channel which we call a "rao" in the Doon.

The Sewalik Hills are covered with dense jungle, the principle trees being sâl, sênd, seesum, jamun, huldoo, and cheer; the two first very hard and valuable wood for building timbers; the third a beautifully dark grained and mottled wood, resembling rosewood, used chiefly for furniture; the fourth and fifth are light, yellowish tinted woods of inferior value; while the sixth is the long spined Himalayan pine, the grain of which resembles deal, but as the tree grows with a curious corkscrew twist, turning as it were on its own axis, all planking or timbers cut from it are cut aslant the grain, and are comparatively weak and useless.

These jungle trees are often overgrown with masses of the maljun, or great elephant creeper, the leaves of which are the favourite food of the sambah, or great-horned stag of the plains, the native name used for this stag is the burra singha, while the twelve-horned deer is bârâ singha, and the names are frequently confounded.

The geological formation of the Doon, and of the low hills and slopes at the foot of the Himalaya is the same as that of the Sewalik; boulders, clay beds, red marl, and variegated sandstone, with saline springs in some places, but the Himalayas themselves show an abrupt change to the oldest limestones and schists.

It is impossible to conceive a more glorious amphitheatre than that formed by the Doon and its boundaries; a valley of five hundred square miles in extent, beautifully variegated by forest and field, the two finest rivers in India rushing past it on either side over stoney beds which break their clear waters into foam, as unlike as possible to their silent slimy course, where crawling saturated with sand and mud through the heat-oppressed plains between their mountain sources and the sea; an ever-changing panorama of hills surrounds the valley, the course of the sun, and the changing lights of cloud and clear sky bringing out or throwing back their variegated peaks continually, while high, and above all, to the northwards, whenever the weather is clear, shine the pure white pyramids of eternal snow.

The rainy season, which is the only disagreeable time at Mussouree, or in the valley, affords to the artist an endless panorama of striking effects in light and shade; the great command of distance given by the elevation of the Mussouree hills, the dense clouds of the rains, the bright sun-light of the East, the broken shadows of the hills, the numberless streams and varied landscape of the valley, form dissolving pictures of dreamland more wonderful than even Turner's conceptions.

It must be remembered that in speaking of the Himalaya, we do not allude to a single line of hills or a Sierra, though that term applies to the snowy range. The Himalaya include the whole of the country between Cashmere and Cachar, and between the plains of India and the plains of Thibet, or Heemachul, the country of snow, as it is called by the Tartars. This tract of territory possesses no table land, properly so called, but is like a gigantic system of ravines, being throughout a series of steep or precipitous acclivities, the valleys descending to narrow gorges and stream beds, the hills ascending only to narrow ridge tops, and again immediate descents.

These hills possess sites for villages at every elevation, from one thousand feet to the highest limit to which human beings have climbed, *i.e.*, little over twenty-two thousand feet, they present therefore corresponding varieties of climate, and a flora and fauna equally varied. An accurate observer is able, with but a short experience in the hills, to tell pretty nearly the elevation of any spot above the level of the sea, by noting the species of trees and plants which are indigenous at it.

As a matter of course, hunting in the hills themselves can only be followed on foot, and it is by dint of practice alone that any one unaccustomed to precipitous ground can traverse fearlessly the airy-looking pathways, or scramble over the dangerous and pathless cliffs which must be scaled in gooral or thâr shooting. The faculty, however, of looking over a precipice, or having a good head for what a plainsman would consider bad ground is very soon acquired, and a stranger who has been roaming for a week only about the Himalayas, is surprised at his own timidity on first arrival in places where he can afterwards see no danger.

Nervous persons sometimes assert that having "bad heads" they never lose their dread of difficult ground, but this arises chiefly from their always avoiding anything like a difficult place, or, striving, as they ought, to gain confidence by practising on comparatively easy ground till they can take more advanced lessons.

A light pole, about six feet long and the thickness of a billiard cue, increases much the safety and confidence with which difficult places can be passed; but by far the best plan where the sportsman finds himself growing timid from losing confidence or footing is at once to take off the shoes; this will frequently restore complete self-possession, but should it not do so, it is better to lie down and remain measuring distances with the eyes, and alternately closing them for a few minutes, or for any length of time that may be requisite to restore confidence. Want of food frequently produces a tendency to giddiness, and it is as well to take a biscuit or a hard-boiled egg and a native chapattie in the pocket, where a long day's work or difficult ground is to be expected.

The watershed line of the Himalaya is situated beyond the highest snow peaks, which are placed on spurs running south from the watershed. The watershed of a mountain, or of a range of hills is very often adopted as a boundary mark in our hill provinces, and the watershed of the Himalaya divides our territory from Thibet. The crest line of the range which divides all rain water falling on it, by sending all streams on the one side to the Ganges and Jumna, and on the other to the Thibetian bed of the Sutledge affords a clear and permanent boundary, and any disputed point in its tortuous course can be settled by a bucket of water.

The ghâts, or practicable passes over the line of snow are all closed for about eight months of the year, they vary from about 15,000 to 18,000 feet in altitude. It is desirable that sportsmen should time their journey through the lower hills, so as to reach the snow ghât through which they mean to enter Thibet about the time the passes open in June; by so doing they carry splendid weather with them through the hills, and get out of them before the rainy season begins. They will not on their first beat through get anything like the best of the hill shooting, which can only be obtained in perfection after the snow falls; they will, however, pass in Thibet, where there is no rain, the only season in which Thibet residence is practicable for Europeans, and avoid the only season that is disagreeable in our own hills.

The height of the fashionable or gay season at our hill Sanataria are the months of September and October, during which time the dense vegetation which follows the rain renders sporting profitless in the hills and dangerous in the Doon; these two months should be spent after return from Thibet at Simla, Mussouree or Nynee Tâl, or partly at each, and the perfection of shooting in the lower ranges of the hills will be obtained from them after the snow falls in November and December.

To repeat an abstract of the best seasons for each district or altitude to be past through, supposing an English hunter to devote a year to the trip, exclusive of the voyage to India and back, which will take about a month each way. Taking the 1st December overland mail for Calcutta, or the big ship round the Cape, if it goes at the time, and can be got to steam twenty miles an hour; and allowing ample time for looking about on the trip up country, the sportsman will find himself by February 12th in the Doon. February, March, and April are the best months for Doon shooting without running either risk from malaria, or inconvenience from heat.

The months of May and June, the hottest in the year, will thus be passed in the hills *en route* from the valley of the Doon to the snow, some experience of hill sport will then be acquired and specimens of nearly all the hill game obtained.

The rains commence in the hills about the 15th June, but by that time the entrances to the snow valleys which lead to the several ghâts should be reached; in them there is but little rain, as their villages have all an altitude of ten to twelve thousand feet. What little rain falls is in the form of Scotch mist, but the clouds, which float about, spoil all sport and render a prompt transit to the other side desirable.

The rains end about September 15th; snow begins to fall on the ghâts in that month, and sportsmen should always recross by the 1st September, and time their march to Mussouree by the 20th. The gaiety of the hill station will be over by the 1st November. All the ladies and officers on sick leave returning by that date to the plains, while the snow becoming general over the hills, makes shooting deserving of the name till the 1st January, when the Doon again, or a new beat towards Cashmere, or return to England are available.

The following are a list of articles which a sportsman should supply himself with in England and India, prior to commencing his campaign.

TO BE TAKEN FROM ENGLAND.

1. A double gun, Terry's breech, fourteen guage, complete in case.

2. A double rifle, Terry's breech, Government bore, complete in case.

3. A Chevalier's binocular field glass.

4. A small hill tent of vulcanized mackintosh cloth, convertible into a boat.

5. One of Mappin's Indian hunter's knives.

6. A spring balance up to 80lbs for weighing Coolee loads, flour, &c.

7. A travelling lamp and a supply of candles for it.

8. Twelve flasks of powder and two bags of

shot, No. 1 and No. 6, (a portion of this may be taken in the form of cartridges.)

9. Five thousand gun caps and two hundred detonating tubes for shells.

10. A full dress suit, as also shirts for the voyage, and personal adornments according to the taste of the individual may be taken out; but as a sportsman all that is necessary on the ground is:—two suits of brown cotton, two of grey woollen, half-a-dozen Crimean shirts, six cotton shirts, twelve pair of woollen socks, four pair of shoes and a cap.

11. A supply of towels.

12. A few pocket knives, blue glass and gauze spectacles, for presents to Tartars.

13. Writing pad and books, the fewer the better.

The articles to be obtained in India, say at Mussouree, are:

1. A servant's pâl or small hill tent.

2. A bag of five hundred bullets.

3. A portable charpoy or bed, and bedding.

4. Two large and two small saucepans, two light kettles and a frying pan.

5. Duplicate, dishes, plates, cups and saucers, knives and forks, and spoons.

6. A supply of bacon, preserved meats and soups in tins, tea and sugar.

7. Half a dozen milk goats.

8. A cantonniere or sling barrel for spirits, with a little padlock on the bung and cock turned by a key.

9. One of the G.T.S. maps of the locality.

It must be borne in mind that in the hills everything must be carried by men, and must be packed away in the light bamboo leather covered creels which they call "kiltas." About twenty coolees should suffice to carry all the sportsman and a couple of plains servants can require. Each coolee carries a load of fifty pounds, and receives as wages twelve shillings a month. Stores for a six months' trip cost about £20, extra purchases, flour, vegtables, £1 a month, or every expense included, travelling in the hills costs from £20 to £25 per month.

The cost of passage overland to India is £110, living at the hotels of Calcutta ten shillings per diem, and cost of trip up country about £25.

I here annex a list of the game and wild animals to be met with in the cross section I have named, giving the native names by which they are known in that locality, and which, in some instances, differ from their names in other parts of India. In the valley of the Doon and Sewalik we find.

The Tiger.	Bagh.
„ Leopard.	Baghera.
„ Lynx,	Seeah Gosh.
„ Lynx cat.	Seeah Gosh Billee.
„ Leopard cat.	Bughera sa Billee.
„ Tiger cat.	Lukkeer wallah Billee.
„ Pole cat.	Bilao.
„ Bear.	Baloo.
„ Hyena.	Lugga Bugga.
„ Jackall.	Geedhur.
„ Fox.	Loomree.
„ Yellow fox	Zurd Lom.

The Grave digger.	Bijjoo.
„ Otter.	Ood Bilao.
„ Elephant.	Hathee.
„ Wild hog.	Bunêla.
„ Porcupine.	Say.
„ Great stag.	Sambah or Burra Singha.
„ Twelve-tined deer.	Bara Singha.
„ Spotted deer.	Cheetul.
„ Hog deer.	Para.
„ Four-horned deer.	Dodur.
„ Barking deer.	Kakur.
„ Hare.	Khur Gosh.
The Peacock.	Morela or Mohur.
„ Floriken.	Churhuj.
„ Barndoor fowl.	Moorghee.
„ Silver pheasant.	Kaleej.
„ Black partridge.	Kala Teethur.
„ Grey partridge.	Teethur.
„ Common Quail.	Buthêr.
„ Rain Quail.	Bursatke Buthêr.
„ Bush Quail.	Lowa.
Various ducks and teal.	Buttuk and Moorghâbee.

The Bara Singha though plentiful to the eastward about Burmdeo is almost extinct in the Doon. In addition to the above which I know to be in the Doon, I have heard of Neel ghai being seen, also the bustard floriken which is rather larger than the true floriken and exactly like a small bustard; also the bastard floriken or leekh, which is recognized by a pair of curious looking pendulous green feathers hanging from its throat.

In the ranges between the Doon and the snow are :—

The Himalayan chamois	Gooral.
,, Goat antelope.	Surrow.
,, Hill stag.	Jurow.
,, Barking deer.	Kakur.
,, Great wild goat.	Thâr.
,, Musk deer.	Kustoora or Bena.
,, Tiger,	Sher or Bagh.
,, Leopard.	Baghera.
,, Black bear.	Baloo.

The Dingo or wild dog.	Junglee Kootta.
,, Hill fox.	,,
,, Pine martin.	,,
,, Forest martin.	,,

The Silver pheasant.	Kaleej.
,, Blue do.	Moonal.
,, Brown do.	Cheer.
,, Mottled do.	Koklâs.
,, Argus do.	Loongee.
,, Red-legged hill partridge.	Chikor.
,, Francolin or black partridge.	Kala Teethur.
,, Grey partridge.	Teethur.
,, Wood do.	Pewra.
,, Woodcock.	Bun Chaha.

In the snow and beyond it on the plains of Thibet :—

The Wild Yak.	Bunchowr or Brong.
,, Ovis ammon.	Nyan.
,, Snow Sheep.	Burrul.

The Wild horse.	Kyang.
,, Snow leopard.	Sufêd Bughera.
,, White ounce.	Chota Bughera.
,, Snow wolf.	Chanko.
,, Snow marmot.	Pheea.
,, Thibet blue hare.	Chasa.
,, Snow pheasant.	Hunyal.
,, Snow partridge.	Burfke Teethur.

CHAPTER II.

ELEPHANT HUNTING.

Wild Elephant sign.—Sir Emerson Tennant's opinions and Ceylon sport.—Hopelessness of riding down Elephants in the Doon.—Characteristics of Doon Elephants.—Elephant killed in the Hutnee Rao.—Khoonnee Elephants and the murderer Gunesh.—Morbid propensities for mischief when "must."—Trapping Wild Elephants.—Pitfalls and noosing.—Elephant language.

WHATEVER may be the kind of game which the hunter in the valley of Dehra Doon pursues, and whatever the direction he may take through its forests, he cannot fail to notice strange pathways marked out, not only through the more level lands of the valley, but meandering over the crests of the Sewalik hills, verging the edge of boulder precipices, and sometimes slanting along the sides of ravines where horses and tame cattle could scarce find a footing.

Long before I had solved the question of the formation of these paths, I had imagined various supposed causes for their existence. The possible tenancy of the great jungle amphitheatres of Sewalik by villagers, or encampments of woodcutters and hunters, or the transit of droves of grain-merchants' bullocks over them ; but every theory of the kind was refuted by the number and labyrinthine involutions of the pathways themselves, leading nowhere but to endless entanglements of creeper jungle, and raviny solitudes. When better acquainted with the Doon and its inhabitants, I ascertained that the mysterious paths of both forest and fell were made by wild elephants, and in the broken land of the Sewalik, a track long lasting is often traced by a single transit of these giant denizens of the jungle.

The entire neighbourhood of the Doon, and the Damun-i-Koh, or skirts of the mighty Himalaya, are admirably adapted for the habitat of the wild elephant—great herds of which go voyaging about in Indian file, leaving a track on plain land of about four feet wide. On hilly ground they keep close to the line, and their pathway is not more than two feet broad, the breadth remaining much the same whether the herd amount to seven only, or seventy. On plain land their soft soles merely press down the grass, leaving a smooth flat path, without cutting the soil; and the dense growth of rank grasses during the succeeding rains, obliterates all trace of their roadway. The amount of attention which they may have bestowed on the neighbouring trees, marks the speed with which they travelled; if alarmed, or journeying to some particular point which they may wish to visit for forage, they do not pluck grasses and leaves, or break and strip branches and bark of trees, as they commence doing when their walk subsides into a saunter. While near the scene of their midday siesta, the main trunk line of their journey breaks off into numberless single tracks, as each goes foraging for himself, though never straying, except in the case of the old male leader, far from the main body of the heard; while a single shrill note of alarm brings all, except perhaps the sulky and independant old tusker, who owns the herd and is conscious of his enormous strength, into a dusky crowd, whence every proboscis is raised aloft, carefully scenting and analysing each breath of air which reaches them, and getting gradually reassured, despite even suspicious sounds and sights in the neighbourhood, if no unwonted odours or human taint offends their olefactories.

Long before I knew by practical and ocular experience that large herds of elephants frequented the Doon, when tracing the annual elephant tracks of the plain, or the perennial causeways marked by their wanderings amidst the broken boulder formation of the Sewalik Hills, I have deemed the colossal game which could range over our comparatively limited amphitheatre, yet remain invisible to our unpractised search, as almost mythical monsters whom I had little chance of ever meeting. I remember, on one occasion, an old officer who had lived for some years in the valley, describing to several younger hands, and myself among the number, a herd of about seventy elephants which he had seen when on duty by one of the Doon water courses. An incredulous glance went round the audience on hearing of such a number, and we afterwards in conversation agreed that old K—— used a more primitive weapon than a rifle in his hunting episodes. Experience has since, however, convinced me that our self-sufficiency was more faulty than the old man's veracity.

The resident sportsmen, and invalid officers located in the Doon and at Mussouree, appear to interest themselves but little in the habits of the largest of Indian game, though many of them are keen and untiring sportsmen in the pursuit of spotted deer, or mahseer fishing.

Invalid officers, by the bye, I found as a rule, to be hale, rosy-cheeked fellows, whose ailments must, like the elephants themselves, have required a practised hand to discover.

Since writing the following account of Doon elephant hunting, I have had an opportunity of reading Sir Emerson Tennant's admirable description of the elephant catching in the Ceylon Corrals as the Kheddas there are called. His personal experience as to the habits of wild elephants, appears to have been limited to the instance of which he so graphically describes the capture of two successive herds in the Corral. His strictures on the notorious case of cold-blooded butchery of an elephant by Gordon Cumming, so often quoted against sportsmen from the "Hunter's Life in South Africa," all true sportsmen will approve, and appreciate his sympathy for the calm dignity of despair with which the wild elephants in the Corral resigned themselves after being bound; but he appears carried away by his subject, and exaggerates both the amiability of the elephant, and the heartlessness of sportsmen. Seated with a number of companions on a comfortable platform, fastened in a group of trees, the size of which ensured absolute safety, Sir Emerson viewed a herd of elephants driven into an elaborately prepared enclosure, some three thousand natives, and a number of domesticated elephants assisting, and every appliance of science and art employed to prevent danger, and render the wild herd comparatively powerless. After describing the ease with which, acting on their fears, they were driven by shouts and clamour, drums, tomtoms, blazing torches, and a hedge fire of musketry into the Corral, and the facility and dexterity with which the noozers, protected by decoy elephants, bound them to trees; he concludes, page 371, vol. ii.

"On the whole, whilst the sagacity, the composure and docility of the decoys were such as to excite lively astonishment, it was not possible to withhold the highest admiration from the calm and dignified demeanour of the captives. Their whole bearing was at variance with the representations made by some of the sportsmen, who harass them, that they are treacherous, savage, and revengeful; when tormented by the guns of their persecutors, they, no doubt, display their powers and sagacity in efforts to retaliate or escape; but here their every movement was indicative of innocence and timidity."

This, I should say, was very likely; but it is very natural that a sportsman, accustomed to wander alone, or with, perhaps, a single attendant through the forest, and trust to his rifle alone when tracking a Tusker, or Rogue elephant, should give a different account of his feelings when face to face with his giant quarry.

I never could conceive what satisfaction some Ceylon sportsmen find in slaughtering a number of elephants from a herd, in a country where tuskers are so scarce that "not more than one in three hundred has tusks."* Not only are tusker elephants so scarce in Ceylon, that, throughout the descriptions and illustrations old Baker's elephant killing, no case of his success with a full-grown tusker is recorded; but the natives will not touch the flesh of the elephant, and he could not even

* Rifle and Hound, p. 11.

have the satisfaction of knowing, as Gordon Cumming did, that by his battues, he was supplying food to scores of half-starved indigenes.

I started one day from Dehra for Dooeewalla, beyond Lucheewalla, with C. Grant, of the Civil Service. Our tents were pitched on a grassy plain dotted with thorn bushes and a sprinkling of jungle trees; we had pad and howdah elephants with us, intending to beat for general game. We commenced beating on the Lucheewalla plain in the direction of the Sooswa river, and had shot a hog deer and cheetul, and started a very heavy pig, when I perceived two great slate-coloured carcases in front of us, which I at first supposed to be rhinocerosses; on nearer inspection they proved to be young elephants, ten years old, who started off on viewing our line. We headed them and followed for some time on foot, and I got a shot at one with a light single rifle, the only one I had with me at the time. I was anxious to secure one, if possible, as it was the first time I had seen them;

but would not, if I had had a little more experience, have thought of firing at such little tuskless animals, as I made it a rule never to kill game of any kind, unless some definite object was to be gained by it. On this occasion, I learnt at least a little as to the speed at which wild elephants can get over the ground when doing their best. No runner, however fast, could hope to escape an elephant by speed of foot, as they will, for two or three hundred yards, keep a horse at a sharp canter. Believing, however, that it might be practicable to "ride elephants" in the Doon, I next day took out a favourite horse, a chesnut, thorough-bred water, named "Waverly," and determined, if elephants were not met with, to practice a run after cheetul or para. Starting after breakfast with Grant, I had wounded a spotted buck in the foot, and, thinking it a good opportunity to test the ground, got off the elephant, and was soon striding after it on Waverly.

I found that the boulder spread scrub jungle of the Doon made such a race more than sufficiently exciting, to say nothing of the numerous dry nullahs, too much concealed with bush for the banks to be seen plainly, and too wide for any horse to clear, even under favourable circumstances of ground. As I flew past trees, and dived below branches, gaining at every step on the buck, I felt sundry ominous trippings of my horse's feet, as they broke through heaps of boulder stones and earth, the irregularities of which were entirely concealed by grass and bushes. The farther we went, the faster the pace became, and the worse the ground; but, as a few more strides would place me alongside of the chase, I urged Waverly on, thinking each stagger or stumble would be the last, and, stretching over his neck, was pointing my revolver at the deer's heart, when, with a fearful crash, Waverly pitched on his head. I, of course, imitated him successfully, and, after a complete somerset, the horse lay with his flanks on top of me, the holsters and saddle-pummel crushed, and myself senseless.

How long I lay there I don't know; when

I awoke, I found Waverly standing over me with a vacant countenance, and most dilapidated general appearance, while, for five or ten minutes, I had myself but very vague notions as to my own personal antecedents. I soon managed, though much shaken, to remount, and rode back to the line of elephants, fully satisfied of the impracticability of riding down elephants, or any other game in the Doon, and retaining in my side, for some weeks, painful reminiscences of my tumble.

Some time after the above bone-shaking purl, I heard, through certain of my native subordinates, that an elephant had taken up its quarters near one of the dry torrent beds of the Sewalik, called Hutnee Rao, near Kansrao, a well known camping ground, on the road between Dehra and Hurdwar. As is usual when such reports are made, this particular elephant was described as being of Mammoth size and portentous presence, alarming to even more than the chronic state of Elephantaphobia all wood-cutters and brinjaras in that quarter.

While in the valley, my official duties seldom permitted my taking advantage of information of the kind, as I could only leave the office and treasury during native holidays, or when on duty in the interior, and my assistant on duty at head-quarters. On this occasion I had to ride out in the evening, hunt all next day, and return at night. I had in the meantime obtained the skull of a Commissariat elephant which had died in the jungle near Dehra, and sawed it in two to examine the position and size of the brain, and the inclination and strength of the bones of the head.* Gordon Cumming says, if I remember right, in his work on African hunting, that it is useless to fire at the head of the elephant, as no ordinary weapon can ensure penetration, and it took him an average of about thirty shots to kill each elephant, firing chiefly behind the shoulder. Indeed most sportsmen seem to be agreed as to the head shot. In Mr. Charles

* Vide plate containing longitudinal section of an Asiatic elephant's skull.

John Anderson's interesting work on South Africa, published by Messrs. Hurst and Blackett in 1856, the following note is given as to "where to aim at an elephant." "I lost many noble beasts from the small calibre of my guns, which did not carry more than fourteen and seventeen balls respectively to the pound. This was more especially the case as regarded the elephants; and it was not until after a time, and when they had become scarce and shy, that I found out the way of bringing them down with any certainty at one or two shots. I found the best part to aim at (when shooting by night) was the shoulder, either behind or in the centre, near to the lower edge of the ear. Another good point, provided the gun be of large calibre, is to fire at the leg, which once broken, the animal, in almost every instance, is completely at the mercy of the hunter."

But Ceylon sportsmen, on the other hand, kill numbers of the Ceylon elephant by single bullets from ordinary rifles, firing through the forehead or temple to the brain. The opinion of Mr. Baker, the first of Ceylon elephant hunters, I have quoted in Chapter XII.

The African elephant I know to be a distinct species from those of the Doon Valley, the Ceylon is more of the Asiatic type, but doubtless a variety, as there are marked characteristics by which even the elephants of the Dacca, Kheddahs, and Assam are distinguished from those of the Doon; the latter has all the "points" most valued by a hunter, in choosing Shikaree or Suwaree (*i.e.* hunting or riding) elephants; they have a highly arched back and bowed legs, the appearance of bandiness being given by the large amount of muscle on the exterior part of the fore leg or arm. The slope of the forehead and trunk, or facial angle, is nearly perpendicular, not receding and swinish as in the Assam kind; the colour of the skin is very dark, and the species is known to the natives as the "Kalabuns."

Wild elephants always appear a much lighter colour than tame ones, from their keeping themselves covered with either mud which drys to a yellow or blueish colour, or dry dust; they do this as a protection from the bites of flies to which they are extremely sensitive, and which cause them great annoyance immediately after the rains.

I had not, at the time I heard of the big elephant of Hutnee Rao, any guns well adapted for elephant shooting; being very fond of rifle practice at a target, and adopting the American principle of very small bores, with heavy metal, my rifles, though well calculated for match shooting, were many of them almost useless for heavy game. I had therefore a conical bullet, with steel tip, adapted to my single barrel duck gun, and took a common 14 guage double barrelled smooth bore loaded with ball as a reserve. The comment of one of my friends on my preparations, was that I might as well shy my hat at the elephant, he would probably dance a double shuffle on the top of me as a finale to the episode of attack. Acting, however, on the Khubur, or information I have alluded to,

I rode out to Kansrao, where I found an old friend, Major Hampton, of the 31st. N.I. encamped; he lent me an Arab charger, who would stand fire, to ride the next morning, though I knew from experience that following game at speed, or fighting from it, would not be practicable on the slopes of the Sewalik. A Brinjara guide, and a little Ghoorka Shikaree, who carried my second gun, accompanied me. On leaving the bank of the Sooswa, we passed through Sâl and Send forest; the trees much scattered, and the plain rather bare from the grass being burnt, or eaten down by cattle. As we approached the Sewalik hills themselves, and entered the Amsôth and Hutnee Rao, two torrent beds just east of the spot marked as the Forest of Boolawalla in the map, we found a dense forest of young Sâl trees and rank grasses, through which it would be impossible to ride a horse, or run quickly on foot, but which an elephant could crash through at top speed. Here the guide suddenly stopt, and, with elongated visage, pointed to the great flat footmark of a large male elephant. Twice round the fore foot is the measure of the height of a elephant, and the impression of this foot gave the height of its owner as nearly twelve feet. The track was quite fresh, and the broken twigs and leaves around unwithered; the solemn silence of their movements, however, render it very difficult at times to follow elephants through tree jungle, as an incautious advance might change the pursuer into the pursued, and a few sudden changes of direction where the ground is covered with fresh traces, sometimes throw out even experienced trackers.

We wandered far among the wild gorges of the Sewalik without sighting the object of our pursuit, at one time losing all sign of the "koj," as the natives call the foot tracks, and at another coming on the fresh couches where two or three monsters had rolled about or slept. We at last lay down tired out by heat and want of water, which is very scarce throughout the summer in the northern courses of the Sewalik range, when the silence around was broken by the sharp crack of a breaking branch; we went softly and silently in the direction indicated by the sound, and came on a herd of seven large, and several small elephants feeding; they had not scented us, though from inexperience I had taken no precaution on the subject, and were flapping their large ears, and browzing on the surrounding bamboo bushes and other trees. The Brinjara here seeing me lie down to watch the herd, looking out for a tusker, incontinently volunteered his advice that I should rush forward and shoot one, and proceeded to dilate on the necessity of being fearless and firm on the occasion. Placing him at a safe distance, and directing the little Ghoorka to keep about twenty or thirty yards behind me with the spare double barrel, I commenced stalking up to the herd with the single duck gun, when some veer of the wind caused a number of trunks to be thrown up in the air. The trunk has a curious little digit finger attached to it, and in a second each of them was directed to the bush behind which I lay, marking the spot whence they scented danger. The body of the herd then commenced slowly moving off, the fact of their frequently coming across woodcutters in the jungle, rendering them less alarmed than they would otherwise have been. Not a single tusker was to be seen among them, and if the male was not secluding himself at some distance, the head of the herd was possibly some large Muçkna, or tuskless male elephant.

A large female was pulling away at the branches of a bamboo bush, a short distance in front of me, and running forward under cover of it, I got within four paces of her before she saw me, and fired directly into the temple. I had determined to go down the most precipitous bank I could find if my shot did not prove fatal, and started back directly I fired to where my Ghoorka Shikaree was standing within thirty paces of us. A tremendous crashing of trees followed the sound of my gun, and I caught sight of the brinjara who had just been giving me such valorous counsels, flying across country in a horrible fright.

As I was unpursued, I returned, as soon as the herd had cleared off, to the spot whence I fired, and saw the elephant lying dead a little way down the bank, whence it had rolled when shot. The bullet had penetrated the skull, but only just reached the brain, though weighing four ounces, with a steel tip, and I had loaded with six drams, or about four ordinary rifle charges, of powder. Even this charge, however, I found on a later occasion, had no effect, if the thinnest parts of the skull are not chosen when taking aim, and a gigantic single tusker, at which I fired from a distance of twenty paces, after appearing a little dazed or stunned for a few seconds, walked on again as if nothing had happened.

I managed with great difficulty to have my first elephant skinned, but could get no native tanner to attempt to cure even a portion of it for experiment; they gave me the usual logical reason for not trying what they could do, that their "bap dada," (fathers or grandfathers) had never cured elephant skins. The tusks were wretched little discoloured stumps. Having thus proved the possibility of shooting Doon elephants with single bullets, like Ceylon ones, I made a vow to fire no more at tuskless males, or females, unless they were khunnees, or murderers, as all those are called by the natives which have been known to kill human beings.

As the male who heads the herd will seldom allow any rival to remain near it, there are a number of bachelors both with and without tusks, known as solitary males, or single gentlemen, who are often very sinister brutes; they grow savage at certain seasons when "must," as the natives say, or drunk (with love not wine), and sometimes kill all they meet or can catch for a week or two, becoming, however, quiet and comparatively harmless when they return to their sober senses.

There is a solitary elephant which frequents the Doon, known by the name of "Gunesh." This animal belonged at one time to the Government Commissariat, but killed its keeper and escaped to the jungle with a piece of its chain still attached to its leg. The wild elephants keep their tusks in order, polishing the points against trees and clay banks, and the cool and shady savannahs which they frequent, preserve them from splitting, as the tusks of tame elephants do, from their exposure when labouring in the sun, and to prevent which, about a foot to a foot and a half is always sawed off, the end being then bound with a brass or iron ring. This cutting of the tusks, and the short chain which he always drags about with him, mark Gunesh whenever seen. He is said to have killed fifteen people during the same number of years along the foot of the hills.

On one occasion, when a predecessor of mine in the Superintendency of the Doon was encamped at Rajghat by the Jumna in the western Doon, his dawk peon, or letter carrier, was attacked, while quietly running along the road with the letter bag, by a rogue elephant, who came after him from a considerable distance, and crushed him to death, apparently from mere wantonness and cruelty. The widow of the man was allowed a pension of half his pay by government, as he was killed in the performance of his duty. This murder is one of those attributed to Gunesh, I was never able to come across him myself; and a party of nearly three hundred Simooree Ghoorkas once sent into the Sewalik after him when he had committed a murder, failed in finding him, which is not to be wondered at, however, considering that he has a range of many hundred miles of uninterrupted forest and jungle to roam in along the foot of the Himalaya.

While I was at Mussouree, a Commissariat male elephant which had been for some days fractious and troublesome, without, however, any proofs of its being dangerous, was taken by its mahout to drink at a water course passing through the town at Dehra, where numbers of natives fill their pitchers. An old native woman happened to come near the elephant while drinking, and was filling her ghurrah, or eathern jar, with water, when from some unaccountable motive of mischief, the elephant passed his trunk round her waist, lifting her off her legs and putting her under one of his own feet, with which he instantly crushed her to death; but went on wagging his ears and drinking as if his little practical joke had been a harmless freak of fancy.

One of my native writers, who prided himself on his powers of reporting in English, announced the circumstance and its effect on the public mind, in the following quaint phraseology, which is, however, to some extent characteristic of his class.

"Honoured Sir,

"This morning the elephant of Major R—, by sudden motion of snout and foot kill one old woman. Instant fear fall on the inhabitants.

"I have the honour to be, Sir,

"Your most obedient servant,

"MADAR BUX."

As an instance of the savage cruelty of the

khunnees, or rogue elephants, as they are called in Ceylon, my friend Captain R——, the superintendent of forests, mentioned to me that when the Beejapore water course was being made at about three miles from Dehra, a large solitary elephant which had concealed itself behind a clump of bamboo bushes, rushed out on some native labourers going up the canal. They attempted to escape by flight, but the elephant soon caught up the last of them, and threw him on his face by striking him on the back with his trunk; it then placed one of its ponderous feet on his legs, while it twisted its trunk round his chest beneath the arm pits, then wrenched the upper from the lower portion of the body at the waist, dandling the former in its trunk as it walked along; a line of entrails marking the course it took from the crushed limbs, at the spot it caught him, to the head, arms and chest which it carelessly tossed away about twenty paces from them.

Captain R—— also informed me, that on one occasion two of the carpenters employed in felling trees at a gote, or station, in the Chandnee Doon Jungles felt ill and remained at the shed instead of going to work with their companions. There was also a Brahmin left at the shed who was employed to cook food for the carpenters. One of the sick men went out to a neighbouring spring to fetch water, and as he did not return, the other thought he had grown better and gone to work, so went for water himself, but he also did not return.

In the evening, when all the woodcutters came from their work, they asked the Brahmin where their two friends had got to; and on his replying that they had left him about noon to join their party, some of the natives, with characteristic apathy, announced that they had seen a dead body lying near their path on the way home, but as it did not concern them they had not made any investigation about the circumstance; they, however, now returned, and on reaching the spot found the history of the two men's fate written on the ground and shrubs around.

A khunnee elephant had evidently been

standing near the spring when the first man came for water; the koj, or track of both man and beast, with the doublings and struggles of the former to escape when pursued by the latter were all mapped out. The footprints of the elephant sometimes obliterating those of the man, showed clearly the position of pursuer and pursued up to the spot where the man was caught and where his body still lay. There was no external mark of injury, but a little dust was on the chest, and on feeling the spot, the bones within were found to be completely crushed, life having been destroyed by a gentle pressure of the beast's ponderous foot.

The second arrival had been treated in the same way, and his body was found a short distance off. This will explain the abject terror which the sudden appearance of wild elephants produces, and the apparently unreasonable fright and flight of natives from their vicinity, even when in a herd and comparatively inoffensive.

There are two methods of trapping wild

elephants, practised in the Doon, one by pitfalls, the other with the assistance of their domesticated brethren. In the former, some elephant's path which has been several times traversed during the year is chosen, probably the road from the jungle to some drinking ghât. Several pits, about twenty feet wide and fifteen to twenty deep, are dug in a line transverse to their pathway, and are then covered with branches and grass. These pits are called "ogees" by the natives, and their frequency in former times is attested by their naming many places in the Doon, such as Ogeewallah, Ogee Chokee, &c.

Though these pits are admirably concealed, it is not often that elephants fall into them; they not only try most carefully, when at all suspicious, the ground before them with their feet, but make incessant use of their trunks in testing the ground, or lifting off the pathway any branches or other impediments which might conceal a trap. Government has lately taken the trapping of wild elephants into its own hands, and the officials employed in trapping discountenance their being caught by private individuals; there is not, however, any law to prevent their being either shot or caught by private persons or others; and as they do enormous damage to the rice, sugar, and other crops of the Doon, it would not be just towards the farmers to prohibit their protecting themselves as they best can.

It is a troublesome matter getting the elephant out of the pit after once in, and it is seldom done in India without the help of a tame elephant. A large female named Ram Kullee, belonging to Anunt Ram one of the Sikh mahunts, or chief priests at Hurdwar, was famous for its abilities as a nurse or trainer to newly caught companions. She herself had absconded into the jungle on two or three occasions, but returned of her own accord apparently tired of forest life; the wild and tame one are coupled together, and it is sometimes necessary to place a tame one on each side of the wild animal. If no tame trainer can be procured, it is necessary to starve the newly caught animal in the pit, and accomplish his taming to some extent before he is let out of it, but as full grown males are almost untameable and no domesticated one will face them, it is sometimes necessary to destroy them.

It is marvellous how utterly ignorant a captured wild elephant appears to be of the presence of any human being seated on the back or neck of a tame one near him; the newly captured animals are for a time so savage, that they could destroy anyone within reach of their trunks, and rush furiously so far as their leg ropes will allow at anyone who passes in front of them; but the same person, by mounting, as the drivers do, on the neck of a tame elephant, can go with impunity up to the new comer and noose a foot, or tie on or loose any neck ropes which may be required.

The nooses which are placed on the legs when the animal is first captured, get imbedded in the flesh, as the legs swell frequently, cutting on one side to the bone and leaving marks which last the animal's lifetime. No food is given for several days to the elephant, and the native who is chosen as its mahout or driver, then goes and offers it food of various kinds and eases its leg ropes ; the emaciation produced by want of food and the wounds on its legs reduces wonderfully the animal's spirit, making it what the natives call "ghureeb," and grateful for the attention of its keeper.

The drivers throughout India adopt the same jargon of words or elephant language; their vocabulary only amounts to about a dozen phrases, and the animals very quickly pick up their meaning; indeed I have heard an old mahout stoutly maintain, that the expressions they used were the correct and natural elephant language, and that elephants had an intuitive knowledge of it, understanding when first caught just as well as afterwards.

I give a list of the words, as it is frequently of advantage to the sportsman, especially when bird shooting in long grass, to ride on the neck of his elephant and drive it himself, having a servant on the pad behind to carry his gun and load.

The elephant can be driven and guided by

signs or words, generally a mixture of the two. It has a necklace of cotton cords knotted at intervals which serve as stirrups, a touch of the foot behind the animal's right or left ear turns it to the opposite side, a pressure of the point of the ankus (driving iron) or a common stick against the top of the head urges it on; while touching its forehead, or pulling at the ear with the hook of the ankus stops it; a pull of the ear from the ground with the hand makes it kneel down. The following words are used :—

Mail, (pronounced mile). Get up, or go on.

Baith. Sit, or kneel down.

Dutt. Stop.

Dutt, dutt (repeated). To go backwards, Dug to step over any thing. Sometimes, "Lumba Dug," to take a long step over a ditch, &c.

Turuth. Break, or pull down any branch in the way.

Beree. Leave go, or stop feeding, (when passing through crops.)

Chai. Turn.

Chai Dutt. Turn round.

Elephants are often very badly treated by their drivers, who are generally Mussulmen of the lowest class. The ankus is a heavy iron spike with a hook attached to one side of it, and this hook the drivers, if they lose temper, will sometimes drive, by a blow delivered with both hands, into the cellular boney structure on each side of an elephant's skull. These men, however, often exhibit considerable courage and tact in attending on dangerous elephants, and at times fall victims to the perils of their profession. A sportsman should use every effort to keep his temper with his mahout; the whole of the class smoke hemp, opium, and other narcotics, and in the state of obfuscation which it produces, try the temper of their master considerably. Nothing, however, can be more ludricrous and humiliating, than to see in a case of difficulty the mahout hammering away at the head of the elephant, and the irate Anglo-Saxon in the howdah doing the same on the head of the mahout, in the delusive hope of solving the question, but always making the elephant savage and the driver sulky.

CHAPTER III.

ELEPHANT HUNTING.

Elephantine sagacity. — Government Kheddah. — Hunt at Boolawalla.—Night visit of seventy Elephants at Jubrawalla—Hunting at Night—The white Elephant of Umbarree—Tracking Wild Elephants at Motrowalla—Tusker killed in the Horawalla Forest—Proportion of Tuskers to Maknas—The fatal points for Elephant Shooting—Diagrams of Skulls—Prejudices, ancient and modern.

Some few of the most highly trained hunting elephants show an almost human intelligence in their ready appreciation of the assistance which they are expected to render to their masters. The Delilah like tact with which female decoys will pet and humbug some strong stupid Sampson, whom the Philistines have marked for capture, has often been described. The female decoy, as she is called, moves up by quiet and unobtrusive advances to the side of the old male, and there glances in respectful admiration at his massive proportions and ugly face, until she perceives that his eye has been caught by her figure; she then gently passes her trunk over his shoulders, and head, perhaps places her—hand, I was going to say, but mean her—trunk coyly within his. The gentleman, blinking his eyes and flapping his ears, is quite pleased with a partner who carries on all the conversation by herself, and is ever ready to pass from one wheedling manœuvre to another, perhaps placing the point of her trunk against his lips, or rather right into his mouth, which is the elephant's manner of kissing, before she commences tieing his legs; and it is this last which most clearly proves their wonderful reasoning powers, for the mere flirting and fascination being practised in a natural state, is not so noteworthy as their appreciation of artificial aids, of the nooses and ropes employed by hunters.

The Superintendent of Kheddas, Lieut.

Howell, mentioned a case to me in which a practised female decoy had not only been taught to make the figure of 8, by repeated plies of which the wild elephant's legs are secured, but also to hitch the end of the rope in the last loop to prevent any chance of its getting loose. Making the simple figure of 8 I have heard of more than one elephant learning. Clearing a pathway through jungle, by breaking down branches of trees, or pulling creepers which impede the howdah, is a very common practice with hunting and pad elephants, they seldom mistake the particular branch which obstructs the progress of the line; and I have known a case when an elephant on a tiger shooting expedition, suddenly commenced trumpeting, swearing, and shaking its head, protesting energetically as to the immediate presence of the tiger; but as none of the party could see any trace of it, one of the gentlemen desired the mahout to make the elephant, if possible, show them the animal; and on being addressed with a mixture of objurgation and endearment, in hathee bolee, or elephant slang, it seized and lifted off the ground a quantity of dry brushwood, beneath which the tiger was lying concealed like a cat.

There are in almost all the stream-beds through the serai and jungles, at the foot of the hills, quicksands of sand and clay, called fussun by the natives, into which, if elephants once sink, it is very difficult to extricate them. In a wild state, they always avoid beds of fussun; but as it is necessary in beating tiger grass, to keep the line rigidly, there is sometimes an alarm given of an elephant bogged. All hands immediately assist, if the animal is too far sunk to get out by its own exertions, in removing articles from the howdah, and getting the latter off, while others commence cutting down boughs of trees from the jungle, with hatchets generally kept in every howdah for the purpose; these branches it is only necessary to hand to the elephant, who devines their purport, at once raising a leg as high as he can, placing a thick bough under it, and moving his trunk about with nervous rapidity, to seize the supports as fast as they can be brought to him. He soon makes a causeway for himself to the bank, if there is a plentiful supply of wood; but if there is only grass jungle about, he gradually sinks, making desperate efforts every now and then to escape, while the treacherous clay is engulphing him. The last that is seen of him is the end of his trunk, which he holds up with its curious little digit finger, catching for breath, until it is also swallowed up; and the body perhaps lies embedded till its sand bed turns to stone, and in after ages, the short lived elephant achieves fame and immortality as a marvellously perfect fossil specimen.

While I was Superintendent of the valley of the Dehra Doon, the experiment of trapping was tried for the first time by Government. A young officer of the 2nd Europeans, named Howell, being appointed to organise the necessary establishment, and I thus had an opportunity of seeing hunting on a more gigantic scale than is practised in any other part of the world.

A kheddah is the rough timber enclosure in which elephants sometimes are trapt, but is here applied to the trapping establishment, which consists of ten or twelve Commissariat elephants of different sizes, an equal number of phunnetts, or noose throwers, mahouts, and forage-cutters, also a party of matchlockmen. The kheddah elephants have each a small pad, like a racing saddle, tied firmly on its back; the rope is passed twice round its body and once round its neck, and ends in a large noose. The phunnett, during a hunt, sits on the pad, carrying the noose in his hand, and driving the elephant with his feet. A grass-cutter also clings on by a loop, which hangs from the pad over the elephant's tail, and urges the brute when ordered to full speed, by hammering on its stern with a wooden mallet, from which a few blunt iron nails protrude.

The camp of the kheddah superintendent is constantly moved about, as the sagacity of the wild elephants soon teaches them to dread its vicinity. Any brinjara, or woodcutter, who brings to the camp news of the locality of a herd, and conducts the officer in charge within sight of them, is entitled to a reward of fifty rupees. On one occasion, when the camp was pitched south of the Boolawalla pass, an old brinjara, named Ruttun Sing, came in to announce that a very large herd of elephants was grazing in an amphitheatre of the Sewalik a few miles off. The entire camp was instantly in apparent confusion; elephants being saddled and mounted, matchlockmen equipping and lighting their fuses, and parties being told off preparatory to guarding gaps in the circle of precipitous hills, within which the elephants were to be enclosed. Of course, firing with ball cartridge is prohibited on such occasions, the crowd of attendants always drive off dangerous males, while females or young elephants are to be pursued and caught.

On reaching the spot indicated by Ruttun Sing, a herd of about one hundred elephants of different sizes were found surrounded by steep banks and jungle. The several ghâts where raos entered the amphitheatre, or where the banks were sloping, were occupied by matchlockmen; and the hunting elephants, nine in number, entered the more level space. There appeared to be only two male tuskers with the herd, and not knowing what their conduct might be, Howell directed the largest of the tame tuskers, called Ham, (a name borrowed by Mussulmen writers, and bestowed on the elephant by his mahout) to be moved to the front near the herd; the smaller of the two males which happened to be the nearest to Mr. Ham, immediatcly came down to the charge, striking him on the flank, and the shock not only sent him flying in consternation from the spot, but affected his nervous system for some months afterwards. The herd soon got seriously alarmed; but when attempting escape by any of the regular ghâts, were driven back by the blank volley firing of the matchlockmen; then, as opportunity offered, the phunnets rushing in, managed to noose and drag to convenient trees for tethering, four females and four buchas, or baby elephants, before the herd contrived to break through the encirclement.

When a herd is approached in the open jungle, or without the assistance of any nullah ending in a *cul de sac,* as soon as the older and more wary animals are seen moving away, the pack of tame ones is let loose and a most exciting cross country dance ensues; great dexterity and agility is required in the riders to prevent their being swept off or stunned by branches of trees. The wild herd soon begins tailing off, the weaker animals drop behind, and as the phunnett who first nooses anyone of the height received into the Commissariat department (eight feet) gets fifty rupees reward, and there is great jealousy between the Mussulman and Hindoo phunnetts, they all exert themselves to the utmost.

The instant a phunnett nooses a wild animal, he cries "muddud, muddud," (help, help,) at the top of his voice. If he happen to fix the noose on the slope of a hill, the wild animal, whether noosed by the foot or neck, carries away the tame one at a dangerous pace, for it rushes at once down hill crashing recklessly through bushes and trees. It is the duty of any phunnett within hail, to turn at once to the assistance of a comrade who has fixed his noose, and as soon as two or three additional nooses have been fixed, the wild animal, anchored to as many of his large tame brethren, is helpless.

In the *mêlée* which followed the rush after the elephants, one of the matchlockmen got thrown down and was killed, while old Ruttun Sing was swept off the elephant on which he had been seated. Sitting down violently on the ground from a height of about ten or eleven feet is quite enough to confuse the intellect; he had in his fright when run away with, as he thought, commenced hollowing vigorously "dutt, dutt," which he knew was the elephant lingo for "stop." When found on the ground, he was sitting up solemnly repeating "dutt, dutt;" and long after he was picked up and placed in safety on another elephant, he gravely continued the same formula, which was henceforth added as an additional title to his name.

The buchas, or little sucking elephants, of four or five feet high are ludicrous little monsters; they become troublesomely familiar after about two day's initiation in the ways of civilized life. A stranger arriving in Howell's camp, and proceeding in all innocency to the quarter where the elephants were picketted, would be immediately subject to examination by those inquisitive little brutes. One of them, perhaps, playfully removing his hat, when apparently, phrenologically examining his head; while another, with cheerful familiarity, would make him stand on one leg, by winding its trunk round the other. I have known one of them considerably astonish a gentleman, by insinuating the point of its trunk into his pocket, and the suddenness and facility with which it unbuttoned his pantaloons.

Wild elephants have a wonderful faculty for remembering the exact season at which forage of their favourite kinds is fit for eating in different places. To the right of the road between Dooeewalla and Kansrao, at the junction of the Song and Sooswa rivers is a large bed of the reeds or tiger grass, called "nul" and "nurkut" in Hindostani; this the elephants have apparently declared in their mental almanack to reach the stage of maturity at which it is most agreeable to their palates, about the 12th or 13th February; and to it, therefore, they come year after year at almost the same date, hiding in the Sewalik Hills, just south of the spot, during the day and visiting the nul every night. I was once encamped near this nul jungle on the bank of the Sooswa, which is covered near that spot with a dense bed of water cresses, with my friend Major Ramsay of the Kumaonees. We had several elephants in camp, and about midnight they became very uneasy, giving vent at first to the sharp squeaking noise which is often misnamed trumpeting by Anglo-Indians, the only trumpet which it resembles is the penny article contested for at fairs in the aristocratic game of "Aunt Sally." They soon after commenced the bôl, or resounding bellow, with which the wild animals often shake the jungle, and they were soon afterwards answered first from one point then another of the compass, till the night seemed alive with their voices.

Everyone in camp was soon awake; the natives all conversing in whispers, and placing extra chains and ropes on the feet of our elephants for fear they would break away. There was some danger in thus pinioning them, for if attacked by the wild ones they would, of course, be unable to escape; but if once loose, it was probable that the males would be killed, and the females go away with the herd. Each of the tame ones lost, or injured, would have cost us eight hundred rupees (£80.)

As we tried to peer through the darkness, we suddenly recognised the presence of one great pioneer tusker near our elephants, then moving masses in the neighbourhood seemed to rise and fall. Some large opaque body which we thought a bushy tree and scarce noticed, would slide off in solemn silence, while dim outlines of arched backs and trunks moved before us like the dissolving phantoms of a dream. Suddenly, the main body of the herd in the nul jungle seemed to take an alarm; and we heard a long continued splash as they trooped to our side from across the Sooswa. There was a gap in the bank near our tents which were about one hundred yards from the stream, and as the leading elephants made for this, we soon saw the whole misty column gliding past us in a blue glamour light, as evenly as objects on the slide of a magic lanthorn—a slight crackling sound as of straw breaking, being the only one caused by their transit. There were, I should say, at a guess, at least seventy in the herd, and as I noted here and there the gleam of a tusk, I regretted much that I had not some weapon, such as I have since obtained from Witton and Daw, on General Jacob's principle, the shells from which would have secured me at least a couple of the seventy. As it was, firing would have been useless cruelty, as I could in that light only have wounded them, and possibly have tempted them to execute summary justice for the assault.

The elephants had scared away all other animals from the neighbourhood, and within a few minutes of their departure, the whole camp, amidst unusual quiet, was fast asleep.

I soon afterwards tried, at the same spot, to bring elephants to the camp during the night, by making one of my hutnees (female elephants) bôl, and succeeded so far completely. I had taken up my position under a tree with a couple of heavily loaded guns to await their approach; but when they were within fifty yards of me, a brute of a tattoo, or grasscutter's pony, which was picketted and forgotten near their line of approach, commenced a pas seul on its hind legs—its black blanket, which was fastened round the neck, flew about like a witch's cloak, and two elephants, who had doubtless never seen such a hobgoblin before, fled along another pathway, snorting with terror.

Elephant shooting at night, however, must always be a dangerous and unsatisfactory sport, despite the use of the facilities for sighting, which I have detailed in Chapter V., it is almost impossible to kill them by the head shot, as it is next to impossible to allign in the dark for the brain; and though the use of shells, and firing into the chest may ensure their destruction, and probable recovery when sought for afterwards in the forest, yet the chances are very much against the hunter's escaping with his life if the animal charges him. Elephants see as well in the night as in the day, while the hunter feels comparatively blind, and firing at them without "bagging," often drives them away altogether from the locality, and deprives the hunter of the chance of a fair fight in daylight.

I spent, or rather wasted a good deal of time in watching at night for an elephant still in the Doon, called the Bourè Hathee or ash-coloured elephant, and though I never came across it, I fired into several others without success. I had been reading a work by Herman Melville called the White Whale, and dreaming, as a natural consequence, of a somewhat similar contest with a white elephant, in which contest the rifle of course always misses fire at the most critical moment. I was rather surprised to hear directly afterwards a long account of a white elephant from some of the zemindars. The white elephant of the Doon is not, however, naturally white, I believe, like the specimen worshipped in Burmah, the proudest possession of his sable Highness "the Lord of the golden foot." Any one who has seen one or two tame animals, may have noticed the leprous looking white blotches which appear on their trunks and faces; and from all I could learn, I fancy these spots are confluent all over the Bourè Hathee's body, giving him the whitish appearance by which he is known. He is said to have splendid tusks, and I hope some of my readers may yet find their way to the Doon, and settle the vexed question of his colour by bagging him.

As my visits to the neighbourhood of the Doon after my promotion, depended on the state of my health, and sick leave is only obtainable, except in rare instances, during the unhealthy plains season of the hot weather and rains, I could not choose my own time for elephant hunting. I had, however, got out from England a double rifle made to order by C. P. Swinburn & Son, three grooved, sixteen bore, 36 inches long, and weighing nineteen pounds. This weight which was very great, as compared with the calibre of the ball, enabled me to use heavy charges of powder, as much as eight drams could be fired without inconvenient recoil. At the closing of the rainy season of 1856, *i. e.*, during October, being at Mussouree, I determined to try what could be done in the Doon jungles when the rice was ripening. The first khubur that reached me after sending out my scouts, was of a large male elephant said to visit the rice fields of Motrowalla at night; Motrowalla is only three miles south-east from Dehra. I sent out my little hill tent and a heavy rifle, and a basket of the paraphernalia for making tea; and I slept under a tree close to the spot usually visited, not with any intention of night shooting, which though apparently very successful in Africa does not pay in the Doon, but with a view to following up promptly the tracks next morning. At dawn, the native watchers came to announce that the elephant had paid his usual visit, so after swallowing some strong tea to fit me for a long day's work, I started with two shikarrees on the track, which bore as we expected straight for the Sewaliks.

Nothing can be more simple than elephant tracking soon after the rains in the Doon, the old beaten paths being overgrown with grass and jungle, every step the animal takes, leaves a legible history of the time he past and the pace he went; the freshness, or fading of twigs and leaves, whether broken by his trunk or by accident in passing, the dew swept from the grass in shady places, the amount of water oozing into his footprints in sedgy ground, mud, besides various tests by cropolytic traces, all give speaking testimony as to his movements; and an English sportsman learns in a wonderfully short space of time to distance all natives in the art. The impression of the forefoot is much larger and quite distinct in shape from that of the hind, and it is a remarkable fact that twice round the forefoot gives nearly the exact height of an elephant; thus a foot mark of about 24 inches across, measures six feet round, and gives a height of twelve feet for the owner of the foot. This may be taken as the extreme height to which Asiatic male elephants grow, nine to ten feet being the average for females. We followed this Motrowalla elephant some ten or twelve miles, and at last came face to face with what was certainly a magnificent male elephant, but destitute of tusks; in accordance, therefore, with my previous determination I did not attack him; and on his charging through the jungle at right angles to us, I hurried back to camp and started my things for a place on the Tonse river, called Punditwarree, about four miles north-west of Dehra, from which I had received further khubur.

The farmers of the village of Punditwarree complained that a herd of five or six elephants visited their rice fields almost every night, and that each visit cost them fifty rupees in rice eaten or destroyed. The farmers, consequently, were anxious that I should attack the herd as soon as they arrived, and I was called up five times during the night with news of elephants destroying rice in the fields close by; but, though I always went out in hopes of a favourable opportunity for getting one, I only fired one shot, and though I hit the animal, did not bring it down.

The natives have timber or bamboo frames perched on posts or on trees, as watch-towers, called "machâns," on which they sleep while watching their crops at night. They are placed at a height to protect them from wild animals, and if elephants are in the neighbourhood, the strongest trees are chosen for them; when moving from one field or machân to another, they carry a gigantic torch composed of the stalks of the bâjara or jowâr crops, which smoulder and keep light for a long time, bursting into flame when swung round the head; these are generally speaking quite sufficient to scare away any wild animal, but I have seen a well-trained hunting elephant charging two or three times through a perfect hedge of fire, caused by burning jungle grass.

Next morning early I started to track, and adopted, to relieve me of fatigue, the plan of following up the signs on a female pad elephant, only getting off when the wild ones were sighted; we found the herd about three miles west of the Tonse in the forest of Dholekote. I attempted four times while there to stalk the old tusker paterfamilias on foot, but they appeared to take alarm whenever I dismounted, though gazing apparently without fear on our elephant, which must have appeared to them to have sundry unbecoming excrescences on its back; there was evidently no wind, or, if any, we were to leeward. I therefore determined, despite sundry remonstrances from the mahout, who doubted the power of the rifle to stop a charge, on going up to the tusker and firing at him from the back of the pad elephant. I had a Yankee match rifle, carrying seventy-five to the pound, of which I was extremely anxious to test the power, I fired with it at the tusker's temple from forty paces; and though at that distance I could strike the stalk of a wine-glass, so felt quite certain as to the spot I hit, the calibre proved insufficient, and the tusker set off at a racing pace followed by four more shots from my battery, rather foolishly fired in the vain hope of dropping him. We then commenced tracking again, assisted here and there by drops of blood. After a five mile trace, we found that we had changed the track, having lost the wounded elephant and taken up the traces of one moving away altogether from the herd—that we were, in fact, following the fresh footsteps of an old solitary male, on whose reflections we abruptly intruded at

J. Wolf del. M & N Hanhart lith.

ADDRESSING A STRANGER WITHOUT AN INTRODUCTION

about ten miles from the spot where my first shot was fired. We were now in the forest of Horawalla, which is a sure find for elephants when the rice is ripening. I tried the heavy rifle this time, firing from the back of the pad elephant at about fifteen paces; my aim was not perfectly true, the tusker, when hit, stumbled and came to his knees, or rather to his elbows; but as he bellowed outrageously it was clear the brain was not penetrated. I therefore slid off my elephant, and firing the other bullet direct at his forehead at three paces off, killed him instantaneously, then climbed upon the huge carcase and seated myself in triumph. I was amused to see from Anderson's work on South Africa that he did precisely the same on killing his first tusker.

I had promised a friend at Dehra that, if successful, I would send him a foot that he might try one of Gordon Cumming's stews. I first cut out the tongue with a pocket-knife, and then tried with my hands covered with blood to remove the foot with a kookery, or crooked Nepaulese war knife, which, being very blunt, would not even penetrate the skin. I therefore tried by clasping one hand over the other round the handle, and throwing my whole weight on the instrument to force the point of the blade into the ankle-joint, but the blood causing my hands to slip, they ran, tightly clasped, down the blade; it was well for me it was so blunt, or I should have had no more shooting to record. As it was, the bone of the little-finger saved the rest; but the muscle and nerve being severed, has left but the use of three fingers on that hand for life. The head I got into Dehra with great difficulty next day, and buried it for a couple of weeks, that the muscles, &c., fixing the tusks might become decomposed, and the tusks themselves drawn out. The head should be placed at such a depth that, though completely covered with earth, the tusks remain out, protected, of course, by shade from a tree, or by matting, to prevent injury by the sun. When becoming loose they must be carefully watched, or are likely to be appropriated by some indigenous gentleman of lax morality, or, as the natives style such characters, in Anglo-Indian jargon, a "loose wallah."

The Asiatic species has but light tusks compared with those which are imported from Africa; this male, though full grown, had tusks of less than four feet long, and thirty-two pounds weight; but I have known instances of their reaching six feet in length, and nearly a hundred pounds in weight.

I have heard of as many as twenty-five to thirty male tuskers being once seen together in one of the sôts (deep clefts or gullies) south of the Sewalik; but this is a most unusual occurrence, as it is very rarely that more than two or three can be met with in a day's march. None of the females have what deserve the name of tusks, and many of the males, perhaps about a fourth, are mucknas.

In conclusion, I give diagrams illustrating the proper places and direction for the fatal shots in elephant shooting. Nos. 1, 2, and 3, are from skulls of the Asiatic kind; 4 and 5 of the African; No. 6 from a section in the Kensington Museum, shewing how bullets fired into the medulary substance of the tusk are sometimes found embedded in the solid ivory. These will sufficiently explain the discrepant accounts given by Indian and African sportsmen, as to the difficulty of reaching the brain of an elephant with an ordinary rifle ball, for it will be seen that not only is the bone of the African elephant's skull thicker and denser than that of the Asiatic, but the conformation is such as more completely to protect the brain.

There is a specimen of the African elephant skull now at the South Kensington Museum, and several of the Asiatic elephants may be seen at the College of Surgeons.

If the sportsman supplied himself with the rifle recommended by me in Chapter I., he will command the brain of the animal whenever he can see the head; all that is necessary is to remember the exact position of the brain

1.

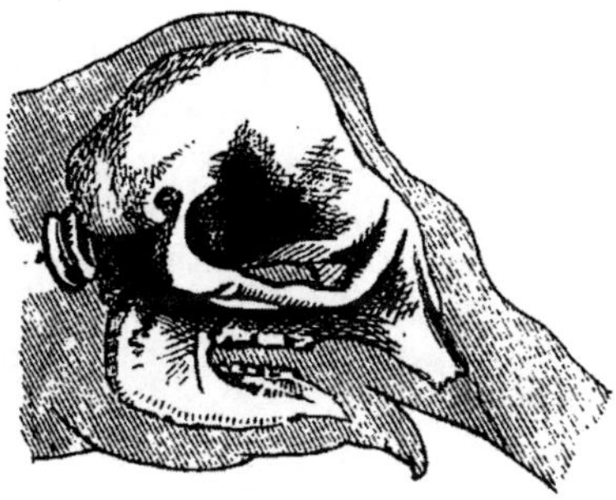

2.

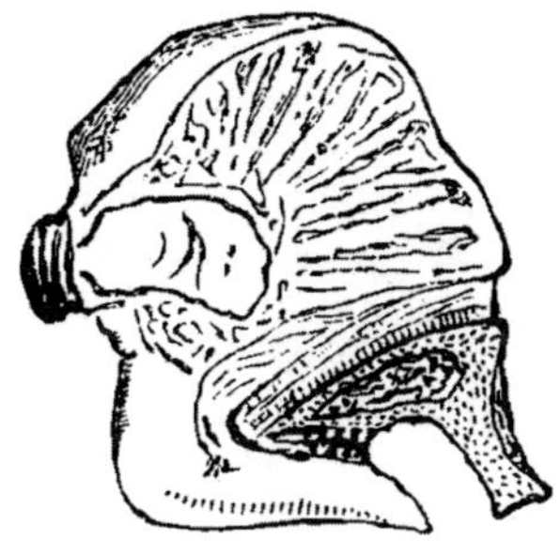

3.

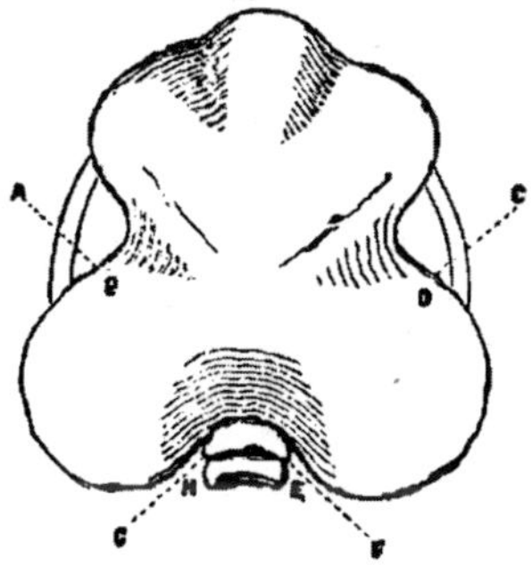

4.

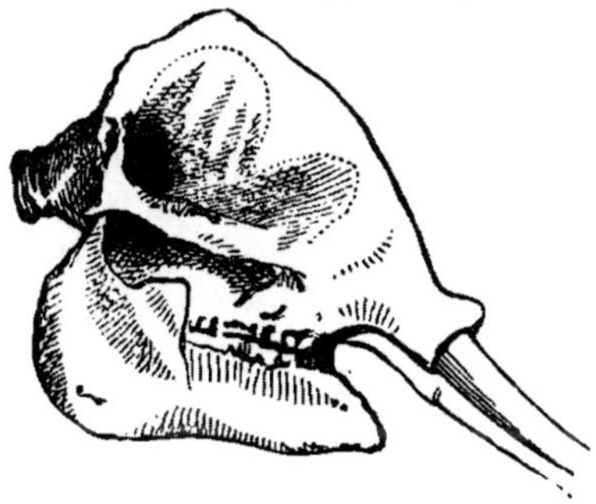

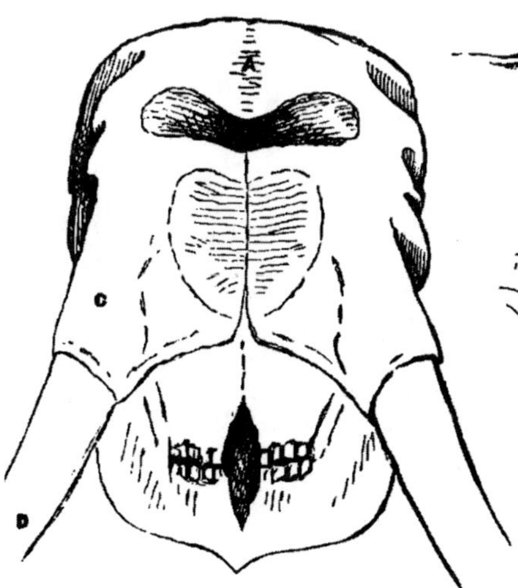

5

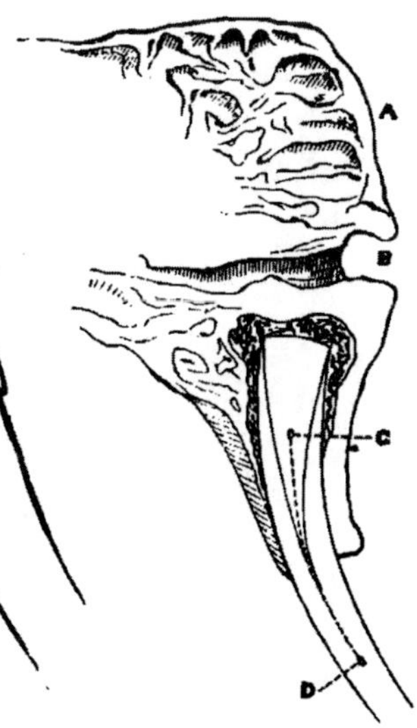

6.

To face Page 90.

and he should allign direct for it without reference to intermediate bones.

When, however, there is time for choice of aim, or for the sportsman to change his position—the best course is to take the right or left temple, shot, marked A.B. and C.D. in diagram 3. This can almost always be obtained by a step or two right or left, even if the animal approaches directly fronting the sportsman. An imaginary line from the orifice of the ear to the eye, if bisected, gives the exact course for the brain. This is the only shot that the sportsman can well hope to save his life by, if the elephant charge down on him, hiding and protecting the brain by curling up the trunk. If, however, with the Asiatic elephant the straight fronting shot offers, the aim should be taken so as just to avoid the lump at the base of the trunk; the skull of the forehead is thick but cellular or spongey, and the shot meets with none of the side walls of bone which are so apt to make it glance, even if it gets through all the muscle, &c., at the base of the trunk.

On a tablet beneath the African elephant's skull, at the Kensington Museum it is stated that the proper shot when fronting the elephant is as if at B in diagram 5 and not at A. When the forehead is very receding or swinish, it might of course be impossible to reach the brain by aiming at the forehead; but under such cirumstances, I should prefer the shot from the right or left oblique (A.B. or C.D. in diagram 3.)

An examination of any skull will explain why Mr. Baker, in Ceylon, found the shot E.F. or G.H. from the right or left rear so successful.

Aiming at the bone of the fore leg is, I believe, under almost any circumstances rather hap hazard work, and I certainly would not like to try it myself.

One of the great advantages of carrying a Jacob's rifle, is that, if provided with suitable shells, the shot behind the shoulder at an elephant's heart, even when the allignment is bad, will destroy the animal with as much certainty as a poisoned arrow. Small animals are struck down with it as suddenly and completely as if struck by lightning; and a shell suited for elephants, *i.e.* the thickness of the copper so regulated that considerable penetration was obtained prior to explosion, would be as effectual as a thunderbolt.

Captain Harris in a foot note to his work on the "Game and Wild Animals of Southern Africa," and Sir Emerson Tennant in his "Ceylon"* quotes the following wonderfully primitive piece of information as to our ancestors' ideas of the manners and customs of elephants and their hunter, from Sir T. Browne's "Vulgar Errors."† "It sleepeth against a tree, which the hunters observing do saw it almost asunder, whereon the beast relying, by the fall of the tree falls also down itself, and is able to rise no more."

That ancient elephant must have been in a disreputable state of intoxication, and hardly deserved a more lengthy report of his case than "drunk and incapable." Knowing as I do, by experience, the strength of an elephant's

* Vol. II. page 292.

† Book I. Chap. I.

head, I would scorn to ascribe the condition of the individual immortalized by Sir T. Browne to anything weaker than whisky toddy.

Quaint and ludicrous as the error pointed to by Sir. T. Browne may seem however, I have, I think, heard of modern fictions almost as faulty. I have a vivid recollection of reading in my schoolboy days of turtles being thrown on their backs, when caught on the sand, or any where out of water, and left there during their captor's pleasure as quite incapable of turning; I was rather surprised, when putting the plan into practice myself, to find that the turtles, if left to themselves, invariably turned on to their flappers again and scuttled off. A turtle if thrown on its back, after a moment or two of quiescence, raises itself a little with one fin, sticks out its head till the back of it touches the ground, then stretches its neck, of which it appears to have an unlimited supply, until it slews itself right again. Another popular notion which I have heard quoted, that the width between the points of the whiskers of any individual of the feline species is the exact measure of its greatest breadth, and used as such by the owner when desirous of stealing noiselessly through jungle to its prey, is one seldom correct as to its premises, and never I believe as to its practice. Nature has beautifully adapted all creatures for their peculiar habits and habitat; there is no chance of any being found who, under circumstances proper to the position in which they are placed by nature, are improperly or insufficiently organized. The breaking of a tree under an elephant's weight, a turtle's rolling from a bank on to its back are likely occurrences without any human strategy; but the elephant in a pitfall, or the turtle on the smooth hard deck of a ship, are not, be it remembered, parallel cases.

CHAPTER IV.

TIGER SHOOTING.

The night moan of the Tiger—Hunting and Death of the Jubrawalla Tiger—A fallacy of the Chinese faculty—Strength of the Tiger—Fighting Tiger killed in the Hurdwar Fair—Best weapon when meeting the Tiger on foot—Take care of his claws and whiskers.

SEATED by the camp fire, or lying awake at night in the Doon forests, I have sometimes heard a deep reverberating moan, low rolling as if along the ground; and as the faint sound of heavy guns at a distance is clearer heard by placing the ear to the earth, or by using an iron ramrod as a conductor from it to the ear, so the ominous moaning sigh, which gives warning of a royal tiger abroad, seems to well up from the ground, hushing all other sounds of the forest, and stopping momentarily even the conversation in camp. The native servants give each other a startled glance of intelligence, and desist from their chatter on the price of grain and ghee, to resume it in whispers directly after on the numberless cases of death and injury their experience knows, caused by the most savage and subtle foe that the sportsman on foot can face in India or elsewhere.

I started one morning with Major R——, of the Kumaon Battalion, from our camp near Jubrawalla, on the bank of the Sooswa, intending to shoot along the Dooeewalla, Lucheewalla, and Hurrawalla plains to Dehra; we had seven elephants with us. There is a piece of land by the Sooswa, just opposite Jubrawalla, which is sometimes formed into an island by a rise of that river; it is covered with young cotton trees, and thick clumps of bair bushes. I can recommend it as a sure find for hog, deer, pigs, and a few peacocks. Just after passing this, we came on the dead body of a bullock partly eaten by some wild animal, the diner on it having apparently but just left it. The ground around was too hard to tell tales by footprints; but we formed line and commenced beating, trusting a good deal to chance, and following along the course of a dry trench partly concealed with jungle, which looked an attractive pathway for any of the feline species. At the first sharp turn in the course of the trench, an animal rose out of it and stood for a second on the opposite bank, within sixty yards of our line. It is wonderful how seldom, except with practised sportsmen, recognition of animals, whose gait and attitudes in a wild state are little known, is instantaneous. On the present occasion, I heard one of R——'s Ghoorkas deliberately pronounce the animal before us to be a calf, carelessly assuming it to be that which he thought most likely to be met with on the spot, though in truth a full grown tigress.

An immediate pursuit was commenced, the tigress taking across a wide open piece of land from which the grass had been burnt. Elephants have a long swinging step, which takes them over the ground at as rapid a pace as a fast trotting horse would go; and in the present instance they were driven by the excitement and emulation of their riders to their highest speed. The tigress being gorged with food, was not in a humour for running fast, so kept just ahead of our line. It was hunting on a gigantic scale, our chase, a tigress, seven elephants for a hunting pack, and scenery to match.

En route, the tigress charged straight through a herd of cattle, scattering them like sheep, and producing a most discordant yelling from the herdsmen. After a run of upwards of two miles, she reached a small patch of jungle, with a deep nullah through it; and as we could not tell whether she would turn and fight, or have sufficient wind left to steal off along it, we took opposite sides, and recommenced beating. I had hardly entered my portion of the jungle, when I saw her under a bush, couched for a spring; and firing a single shot from a smooth bore between her eyes, rolled her into the nullah. She then made several charges up the bank, but failed, apparently confused by the effects of the shot, which had shattered the skull a good deal, grazed past the brain, and caused profuse bleeding from an artery in the throat, where it had made its exit. The shot was a fatal one, as she was unable to leave the place, and R—— coming up directly after, finished her with a ball behind the ear.

The Ghoorkas commenced collecting the brute's fat, when disembowelling it, prior to lifting the body on a pack elephant, believing it a specific against rheumatism. The body was not raised to the pad without sundry remonstrances, in fact, profuse "cussin' and swearin'" on the part of the elephant destined to carry it.

While the body was being skinned that evening in my compound at Dehra, some of the Chinese employed in the government tea plantation at Kaolowghir came in; they ascribe wonderful medicinal virtues to every part of the body of a tiger, and after picking out one bone after another, they ended by getting a cart and carrying off the whole carcase to their own residence.

The Chumars of the Goruckpore district, frequently eat the flesh of the tiger, and thinking that the custom might prevail in the Doon, I asked a Hindoo whether any of his class ate the flesh, to which he rather impertinently replied, that the only natives he ever heard of capable of eating the flesh, were native "Christâns."

Despite the supple, snakelike appearance with which a tiger glides over the ground, when going his ordinary pace, in the excitement of pursuing their prey, for a few bounds, or when charging, they brace up their slouching limbs and tremendous muscles to rigidity.

A blow from the paw of a tiger will strike down a bullock, crushing its ribs, or breaking any bones it falls on. It will then carry off the body, seizing it as a cat would a mouse, and raising itself to its full height by straightening its limbs, will, without any apparent exertion, walk away, scarcely allowing the legs to trail on the ground.

Some idea of the tremendous power of the fore leg of the tiger, can be formed by seeing the matted mass of muscle it contains, laid bare in skinning the animal.

I have never heard a tiger roar, though perhaps it can do so, few persons, if any, have heard what can properly be called a roar. It purrs in the company of its kind like a gigantic tom cat; its cry, heard at night, is generally the low moaning sound I have already noticed. Its charge is accompanied with a succession of rapid startling, coughing growls, but I have heard a bear, when charging, make almost the same noise. I believe the Bengal tiger to be a more dangerous enemy to meet on foot than the African lion; but it is a sneaking animal, it is always trying to stalk or conceal itself and its movements, and never, I believe, indulges in a roar of defiance and indignation like the disturbed lion.

The most extraordinary instance of fearless ferocity in a tiger of which I have ever heard,

Hurdwar in 1855. All readers have heard of the Hurdwar fair. The town and temples are situated at the south-east corner of the Doon by the boundary, but within the jurisdiction of the Saharanpore district. It is at this point that the holy Ganges takes its leave of the hills, or rather is borne to the plains by rushing through the sandstone portals of the Sewalik range; and every year, in the beginning of April, thousands of Hindoo pilgrims, Punjabee Sikhs, Buddhists from Thibet, &c. come to worship—while merchants from Bengal and Orissa, Affghanistan and Persia embrace the opportunity of the religious gathering to effect commercial exchanges. Every eleventh year, called the Koom year, the number who visit the place are much in excess of the annual crowd, the merit of bathing being increased by some system of fanatical progression; and on the occasion I allude to, the crowds at the fair were supposed by officials, accustomed to attend the assembly, to have numbered from two to three millions. A tumult in the midst of so mighty a multitude, or any confusion in the approaches to the principal bathing ghâts would cause enormous loss of life, and the magisterial officials of Saharanpore were nearly all present throughout the fair to maintain order, punish theft, and effect not only the restoration of considerable stray property, but also numerous stray members of family parties who get lost in such a sea of human brings. As the pilgrims were encamped in thousands on the Doon side of Hurdwar, I attended the fair as Superintendant of the Hill district with my assistant, and the usual troop of native officials. Our tents were pitched under some mangoe trees, with the Sewalik Hills and jungle to the rear, but endless numbers of reed thatches and ragged canvas in front; the air being so poisoned by the dense crowd and the impossibility of enforcing conservancy arrangements, as to be quite sickening.

On the second day of our arrival, just after breakfast, a native came running into camp to report that in a wheat-field, a few hundred yards off, surrounded by these dense masses of human life, a tiger had just struck down a man. There happened at the time to be several visitors in camp, viz.: Major Hampton of the 31st N.I., Lieutenant Goddard of the 87th Royal Irish, Messrs, R. Edwards and L. Melville of the Bengal Civil Service, and E. O. Bradford, Esq., now a Deputy Commissioner in Oude, beside my assistant and myself. None of us could believe at first, that a tiger could be promenading in open day without even the shelter of jungle, at a spot where the never ceasing hum of human voices was sounding night and day like billows on the sea-shore, and in the face of hundreds of people.

I had a miscellaneous collection of guns, and could supply one to each of the visitors who were unprovided. We had no Shikaree, or hunting elephants in camp, but sallied forth mounted on three pad ones, with every prospect of a scrimmage worth looking at, as the pad elephants were pretty certain to turn tail, whenever that manœuvre might be most inconvenient to their riders, and make confusion worse confounded if we met a fighting tiger. There were two of us on each elephant, and Bradford rode to the scene on one of my horses, trusting to a riding whip to keep him out of the tiger's reach.

Within three hundred yards of our encampment, we found the unfortunate grasscutter, who had been struck on the head by the tiger's paw, the skull being fractured and the brain protruding, he was in the agonies of death. A little further on, a small patch of broken ground, about twenty yards square with bushes on it, was pointed out to us in the middle of a wheat-field, the young shoots of which were only just springing, and near which there was no jungle. In these bushes the tiger was said to have been lying, when the grasscutter went to cut forage near, and to them it had returned when driven from the body of the grasscutter by the cries of the lookers on.

Thousands of people seeing us coming, gathered round the place, hedging in the tiger with human bodies, and giving us an arena which promised certain mischief from stray bullets during the fight. It was well we were on elephants, for we could fire down on the tiger, whereas if on foot it was perfectly impossible we could have discharged our weapons without doing damage to the crowd.

Our feline friend was evidently roused to a pitch of great excitement, by the expression of public opinion which followed his attack on the grasscutter, and the position in which he now found himself; he did not, therefore, await our arrival, but on perceiving us making for his lair, charged out of his own accord with as near an approach to a roar as he had time to make. The three elephants wheeled round at once and ran against one another, trumpeting, or rather screaming with fright, while Bradford danced round them on my chesnut Waverly; several shots were, however, fired by our quadrille party with tolerable accuracy, inasmuch as none of us were shot, and a ball sent through the fore paw of the tiger which stopt his charge and sent him back to cover.

An active contest now commenced between the elephants and their riders, as no moral or physical force, no coaxing or goading could induce them to approach in line and beat the bushes, whence the ogre issued that had bewildered their intellects; but at last huddled together like sheep, they were edging along about fifty paces from the bushes, steered only by vigorous blows of the ankus, when a second roar heralded a second determined charge. This would have been, from the manner in which it was made, doubtless, a charge home; but fortunately, among the numerous shots discharged from howdahs rolling and pitching like boats at sea, one fired by Melville touched the tiger's spine, and rolled him over within four feet of Grant's elephant, where he appeared lying on his back with hind legs paralysed, to be going through some pugilistic performance with his fore paws. The bellowing of the elephants, the growling of the tiger, and the shouting of the crowd caused a Babel of confusion that made Melville's elephant fairly turn tail and run away altogether.

M & N Hanhart, lith

A PROMPT AND PUBLIC EXECUTION

The cheer which followed the fall of the tiger had hardly subsided, when he staggered to his feet and managed to charge forward principally on his fore legs for a few paces; this he repeated several times when fired at, a rifle ball having apparently a revivifying effect like sal volatile on his system; he staggered up for the last time when some of us were getting off our elephants to take a closer inspection of him. He proved to be a male, and one of the largest I have ever seen.

Soon after our return to our tents, a native came up who had got a bullet through his hand; it had not apparently injured any of the bones, and he thought himself in luck on receiving eight rupees, or sixteen shillings, which is the usual wage for a labouring man for two months. It was fortunate under the circumstances that no worse accidents occurred.

The motion of an elephant running away is indescribably rough and disagreeable; guns, ammunition, &c., are generally rattled about the howdah till scattered over the line of flight, and the riders have enough to do to hold on. The best way of stopping the animal is to send another full tilt after it; the approach of the second has a soothing effect on the nerves of the agitated monster. In tree jungle, an elephant running away may be a very serious matter, howdah and contents are sometimes smashed against thick branches; and the best course for the rider is to catch hold of the first branch he can reach and draw himself out of the howdah by it, leaving his guns, &c., to take their chance, as he will do them no good by getting his own bones broken with them.

In the Teira land, at the foot of the Nepâl hills just north of Goruckpore, I have seen six tigers killed in a fortnight, and we did not kill all that we saw; but it is not often they are met with in such numbers in any part of India. The largest of the six measured twelve feet from the nose to the end of the tail, and that size is, I believe, seldom if ever exceeded, the late Lucknow collection, and which is at present in the Surrey Gardens, says he is thirteen feet and a half in length. Only one of the six tigers was killed by a single ball, and that one only because he happened to be swimming across a nullah at the time the shot was fired, and being cramped by it was at once drowned; the one which showed most fight was a tigress with young, and this is invariably the case.

I consider that no amount of coolness and daring can ensure the life of a sportsman, if he attempts killing a tiger when alone and on foot with the ordinary double rifle or gun. Lieutenant Rice, in an elaborate and interesting work devoted to tiger shooting in the Bombay Presidency, states that a large party of natives, either with or without English sportsmen, say ten or twelve men in all, can pass with safety through tiger grass or jungle when beating, as the animal is always scared away by the noise of many together, but would charge home with certain destruction to some of the party if small in number.

In tiger hunting, however, the conditions of the meeting cannot always be laid down by the sportsman. It is desirable that he should be so equipped, as to require nerve only to render him more than a match for a tiger at any time—and this, modern science enables the hunter to obtain, as the effect of one of Jacob's or Metford's shells bursting in the head or body of a tiger would be to paralyse it at once, as though struck down by a thunderbolt.

Lastly I would warn every sportsman who may wish to preserve his specimens of tiger skins complete, that they must not only be watched most jealously until properly cured, but must afterwards be kept under lock and key until sent out of the country, as the natives will lose no opportunity of destroying the whiskers and stealing the claws. It is quite impossible to prevent this in skins laid out for use or ornament in India; when the tiger's body is first brought in to camp, the native attendants immediately singe off the whiskers, this is partly a superstitious ceremony, but intended also as a grievous insult to deceased. If the natives expect any objection on the sportman's part to their indulging this safe and unaccountably agreeable piece of revenge, they will simply take an opportunity of doing it surreptitiously, and I have known an Englishman quite surprised at the whiskerless state of his tiger skins, when I directed his attention to the fact. The claws are valued as charms by all classes of natives, who make them into ornaments and hang them on their own persons, or those of their children ; and as their loss is not often noted by a European sportsman, his servants have the less hesitation in appropriating them. Give the skin while being cured into the charge of the jemadar, or head servant, and if it is to be exposed or used as a rug in India, take off all the claws and keep them in a cap box till your return to England.

CHAPTER V.

GENERAL DOON SHOOTING.

Beating with Elephants in line—Borrowing Elephants—Carriage in the Doon—Grass Burning—Localities for Cheetul—Average of bag to bullets fired—Caution in aiming at Animals—Beat from Boolawalla to Motrowalla—Locality for Sambah—Locality for Four-horn Deer—Localities for Doon Game-birds—Hawking—Fishing and Fish Shooting—How to cook newly killed Game tender—Portable Machân, or Shooting-box for trees—How to sight with gun at night—The Spring-gun trap—Vultures and their Vision—European Soldiers on Private affairs—A digression on the "unacknowledged necessary of life," and a Military Execution.

A DAY in the Doon, at the proper spot and season, beating with a line of elephants, and firing at all that gets up, is certainly the perfection of tropical sport; the variety of the think, for its inferiority in active excitement to hog hunting.

Two or three sportsmen go out together, and the battery brought from England is lodged in holders expressly adapted for it in the howdah of the sportsman's Shikaree elephant, all necessary ammunition being arranged in pouches round the seat, and a native attendant lodged in the kawass behind, ready to load the guns, if required, when the game is plentiful. A pad elephant between each two howdah bearers is necessary, thus three sportsmen would have five among them. Native nawabs, or Hindoo zemindars who keep several elephants for state occasions, are always willing to have one or two kept free of expence when not required for their own use; gentlemen borrowing elephants, of course pay all charges for their food, as also the wages of the two servants usually attached to each elephant. Government Commissariat elephants may also often be borrowed on the same terms; but they are seldom of any use except for beating jungle, the value set by Government on Commissariat elephants is eight hundred rupees, or £80 for each alike, whether good or bad, and this must be paid if the animal is severely injured or killed; but good Shikaree elephants in that part of India are worth from one thousand to two thousand rupees.

It very soon becomes known whether a sportsman treats the animal well; and though at first they can only be borrowed by propitiating the good offices of those of the district officials, through whom application for the loan of elephants should first be made, it is easy enough after the sportsman has been once out and fraternised with the owners, attendants and animals themselves, to get any number he may wish for. The cost of the keep of each elephant, including servants' wages is £3 per month.

The tents, cooking equipage, &c., noted in Chapter I. as necessary for hill marching, are equally serviceable in the Doon; but instead of a troop of Coolees for carriage, a few camels, say three for each sportsman, are equally efficient, and the hire of each camel is but sixteen shillings a month, every contingency included. Camels can go anywhere in the Doon and travel quickly, but constant delays and difficulties are incurred by using hackeries or country carts for carriage.

When the march for the day, *i. e.*, the site of the next camping ground is determined on, the camp and attendants move off to it by the most direct route, arriving in time to cook dinner for their masters by their arrival in the evening. The line of elephants moves off to some good beat for game, and from it to another, keeping merely the general bearing of the new camp site—so that after shooting all day, the party arrives about dusk at the camp, where the animals killed are quickly skinned and pegged out, and the sportsmen fight their battles over again while at dinner or tea.

I lost many weeks of shooting when first in the Doon, from ignorance of the habits of its wild animals, and the proper localities in which to seek for game at different periods of the year.

The dense undergrowth and giant grasses which the rainy season generates in the Doon, get to be sufficiently dry for burning during January and February, the more elevated or drier localities of course taking fire the earliest. All brinjaras and others owning herds of cattle, are interested in firing the grass, in order to obtain a fresh crop of young shoots for grazing. When the camp happens to be pitched near a long stretch of dry grass on a windy night, it is well worth while for a party to proceed after dinner with torches along a line, to the leeward of course of the tents, and ignite the grass at some fifty different places; the spots fired all unite in a long irregular wave of fire, the flames rising to fifteen or twenty feet in height, in some places roaring and crackling as fanned by the wind, while the reed-like cells of the long grasses explode in numbers, as the air within them is expanded bers of black and green fly-catchers flutter about, awoke by the noise and light, and tempted to prey on the insect life disturbed by the flames. Deer and other ruminants sometimes break away through the jungle, scared more, however, by the presence of the torchmen than the progress of the conflagration, as the frequent repetition of the same fiery programme, renders them generally indifferent to the sight of flames, unless in very close proximity. When the grass is first burnt, however, as some little time elapses before the young crop appears through the ashes, the deer seek cover and food in the Sankote forest, and on the slopes at the foot of the Sewalik. The Sankote forest is at the north-east corner of the Doon, by the Bengala, Rambuha, and Chundanawa streams, and a sportsman should kill, if beating with elephants, fifty head of sambah, cheetul, and kakur, &c., in it during the first week in January.

Wild hog and para, of course, remain where the ground is marshy ; and when the first grass commences growing on the burnt plains, and the forest grass and young shoots are being burnt, the deer return to the ground about Jogeewalla and Beebeewalla, in such numbers, that by the commencement of the hot weather, every patch of covert which is too thick to be seen through, is sure to contain something in the shape of pig, para, cheetul, or porcupine, with occasional peacock, black partridge, quail, and sometimes floriken.

In shooting from the howdah with ball, a very great number of bullets are wasted, and numerous animals go away wounded. Few sportsmen are aware how often they miss altogether in such shooting, unless they try the experiment of counting every charge they use. I have known an officer who was a pretty good shot, and who deemed himself much above the average, who used to say that he bagged one out of every three shots; this however, proved to be a fiction, as on testing the results of a day's shooting over the ground at Dhaloowalla, and Jogeewalla, he found that he had discharged ninety bullets, and bagged five head of game. I have myself been over that ground in April, with a friend, when we each got upwards of ninety shots during the day, but bagged only five and six head of game respectively; we, of course, only count four-footed game on such occasions in the bag. I feel sure, that if shells only instead of bullets were used, much better results would be obtained, as the expense of using shells would prevent careless or random shots being taken, while almost every animal struck would be secured. In using ball, at any rate, the sportsman cannot too early impress on himself the utter folly of firing, as many do, all their lives, at the centre of the body of an animal. The sight should always be taken a little above the point of the elbow, or what is usually called the shoulder of a deer; the head is a much better aim than carelessly firing at the centre of the carcase. A little consideration will show that when the aim is taken at the middle of the body, nothing but an accident can secure the animal; if the ball strikes the spot aimed at, when the deer has its side to the sportsman, it will merely spring forward, and disappear in the jungle for ever, though doubtless it dies miserably ultimately. If the bullet strike behind the central spot aimed at, merely passing through the stomach or intestines, the deer may go ten or twelve miles without dropping. I have known a deer gallop one hundred and fifty yards, though shot clean through the heart, the body being afterwards opened to test the fact; but this was a rare instance. I should advise every good marksman, when he gets a standing shot within one hundred yards, to fire at the head; and beyond that distance, or if the animal is moving, at the chest. Never be tempted by nervousness or hurry to aim vaguely somewhere about the centre of the entire animal.

I parted one morning with Major Hampton, at a place called Boolawalla, *vide* map; he intended returning viâ Dooeewalla and Hurrahwalla to Dehra, while I proposed beating the jungle, with one howdah, and two pad elephants, between the Sooswa and the Sewalik to Motrowalla, whence I could ride in to Dehra. I can strongly recommend this beat, whether on starting from, or returning to the station; there are no villages throughout it, but every variety of shady hollow and grassy plain, and a great deal of the dense young saul tree jungle, so characteristic of the Doon, is to be met with. The howdah elephant I was on was a very steady animal, belonging to the mahunt or Sikh priest of the temple at Dehra; my own being not so well trained, I degraded for the day to carrying a pad. A very slight difference in the want of steadiness of a riding elephant, of course makes a very material difference in the result of the day's sport. When a shot is fired at an animal running, it is not usual to stop the elephant for the purpose, the swing of his step is followed by the sportsman's body, and a snap shot taken, which is seldom effectual except at very short distances; whenever a sambah deer, or other animal, is sighted standing, the sportsman says dutt, which both the mahout and the elephant understand; the former lays his ankus on the forehead of the elephant, to ensure his remaining as steady as possible, while the sportsman takes sight with his rifle. Some elephants when stopt in this way, will persist in flapping their ears, swinging the head and trunk, jerking the tail, or lifting the feet, so as to produce a swaying motion of the howdah, which makes the muzzle of the rifle oscillate about the object, and drives the excited sportsman, who loses some valuable opportunities of bagging fine specimens, half frantic. The mahunt's elephant which I was on, would stand when stopt, for four or five seconds motionless as a statue. I first flushed a floriken on the Boolawalla plain, near the Dhoolkund Rao, but did not follow it up, as it left our course. I next sighted a young spotted fawn, which I killed—a standing shot under a burgut, or banyan tree. I soon after shot a hog deer in some raviny grass west of Dhoolkund. A large herd of cheetul got up all around us in a saul forest en route, and I killed from among them a full sized jank, or male with horns. I then came, in the deeper solitude of the Motrowalla forest, on three fine sambah (the big horn,) of which I bagged one; and a little further on, got two more spotted deer, making a bag of six deer, which is an average day's work in the season for a sportsman acquainted with the best localities.

I found that the best and surest find for sambah deer, the largest and noblest looking species of stag which is found in India, is in the ravines, or broad, dry, grassy channel beds, marked in the centre of the Chandpore forest. In hunting for these animals, the sportsman should take a single elephant without howdah, the pad being supplied with a rest for the rifle, and ammunition bag, and passing noiselessly along these channels, or across the flat stretches of grass jungle sparsely covered with trees, he will frequently come on close cropt patches, where the big horn has stampt his traces, or abraded the bark of the trees around, in peeling or polishing his antlers.

When first seen, this giant deer is probably standing motionless, and though gazing full on the intruder, so apparently unconscious in his gaze, that it is difficult to believe that he is alive; this is the moment to halt the elephant, and take fatal aim at the head or heart. If the sportsman be a tyro, he probably fires a shot or two rapidly and without effect, which will leave the sambah still statuesque, apparently unconscious of sight or sound, while a second after, as if suddenly awoke from a dream, he throws up his head and disappears. Following him at the time, if not wounded, is useless; but in a week or ten days after, a return to the spot will ensure in most cases a second interview with the same forest chief.

There is a great deficiency of water in the Dholkote and Chandpore forests during the hot weather, so that few if any cheetul, hog deer, pigs, or birds remain in them. The sambah appear able to do longer without water than other animals, or perhaps to go further for it; and I have, before learning the characteristics of the Doon, gone for miles and travelled many weary hours through those effective on the plains of Dhaloowala, Jogeewalla and Beebeewalla without seeing a single animal of any kind; the few sambah being scared by the noise of our approach and nothing else existing.

All shooting in the Sewalik Hills is of course very different from that in other parts of the Doon, from the difficulty, the impossibility in some parts, of using elephants. The sportsman, with his double barrelled rifle proceeds alone, or accompanied by a single attendant, moving as noiselessly as he can, and studying the course of the wind when approaching any more than usually likely covert. The four-horned deer, sometimes called the goat antelope, which is a rare animal, is found principally on the Sewalik. Kakur are common, and sambah frequently met with. The natives report the existence of gooral; but this I doubt, as the dodur, or four-horn might easily be mistaken for gooral, which I have never seen in the Sewalik, or anywhere at so low an elevation.

The Kaleej pheasant, and peacocks are

numerous in the Sewalik; great numbers of black partridges may be shot in the Sursown, or mustard oil fields when in flower throughout the Western Dcon; and unlimited numbers of the common jungle Moorghees, the origin of all varieties of the chicken tribe are found in the jungle about Hurrecpore and Khalsee, just above the junction of the Tonse and Jumna rivers.

I have made no allusion to hawking and fishing in the Doon, because unable while there to spare time for either pursuit; but those who have time and are attached to that kind of sport, will find ample opportunity for indulging in the amusement. There are a great variety of hawks procurable in the Hills, the principal of which are the baz, churrett, behree, and shaheen, which are caught with great facility, by means of a net between two straight reeds stuck lightly into the ground, and a pigeon or other appropriate bait placed on the opposite side to that on which the hawk may be perched. On its becomes entangled for a few seconds in, the net, the trappers running up and appropriating it before it has time to get way. Camphor and certain preparations of hemp and spices are then administered to it which produce intoxication, it is kept hooded for twenty-four to thirty-six hours, and after that time appears to have become perfectly tame, or at least fearless of the people about it.

The curlew, peawit, storks and herons are caught with the behree, while the baz is flown at peacocks, hares, and even at antelope in the plains. The disappointments, difficulties and comparatively trifling results however, which attend hawking, make it, so far as my experience goes, a most unsatisfactory class of sport.

On the other hand, the fishing of the Doon is excellent, as good as any in the world; the Ganges and Jumna, as also some of the smaller streams, during the rains are full of mahseer, the salmon of that part of the world; it is a finely flavoured fish which yields excellent sport, and grows to an enormous size, the small mahseer are better for the table than the large and coarser ones. Five seers (or ten pounds) is a small fish, eighty pound weight is not an uncommon size, and I have heard of specimens of hundred pounds weight. These monsters are usually taken with spinning tackle, and with lines so strong as to stand the chance of the bait being gorged by the gowch or freshwater shark, which attains, near Hurdwar, to one hundred and ten, or one hundred and twenty pounds weight. The mahseer do not leave the stones, being unknown in their favourite rivers, as soon as the latter pass over the mud and sand beds which commence a few miles from the foot of the hills. Within the hills themselves, after the subsidence of the rains, the large pools formed by eddies and bends in streams are left full of very large mahseer which may be easily shot either with conical ball, or one of Reilly's air cane harpoon throwers, wherever the banks are sufficiently precipitous to allow of shooting down at about right angles to the surface of the water. The plan enunciated by Whitworth and alluded to in my last Chapter, would, I believe, facilitate this kind of shooting.

I have seen some fine specimens of mahseers killed with ball, and also numbers of the anwâri, or mullet, which often swims along the surface of the water with eyes projecting above it like a frog's, killed with the common shot gun. As soon as the mullet is struck, if even with a single pellet of small shot, it appears stunned, and turns on its back; but, as it begins sinking at once, it is generally lost if not immediately seized by some native attendant. The anwâri is the finest flavoured fish which I have tasted in India.

While referring to the flavour of fish, I would point out a very simple plan for ensuring tender meat, and baking it in the jungle. It is not generally known that if the flesh of any animal is cooked directly it is killed, so promptly in fact that the heat of roasting or boiling will warm it before its own animal heat has left it, it remains perfectly tender. Several days of keeping or hanging are required only for the purpose of removing that toughness and rigidity which newly killed meat acquires when cooling. Suppose then a wild fowl or a porcupine shot in the neighbourhood of the camp, which is always supplied in the Doon with a blazing wood fire; the first thing to be done is to cut and wash out the trail, or gralloch the porcupine, while an attendant mixes up some clay and water into a thick paste, which is quickly smeared all over the animal, the quills or feathers giving it a firm hold. This strange looking mud pie is then laid in the fire, which first dries and bakes the mud covering into a seamless earthern vessel, which retains the juice of the meat while baking; some experience is requisite to determine the time for removing the dish and placing on the table or the ground, when a blow with a tent peg separates the case with its quills and feathers, and gives access

I have alluded to night shooting in the Doon, and its unsatisfactory character as applied to elephant shooting; but as it is sometimes useful for tigers, I describe a convenient portable muchân which I had made in the Doon. It is, of course, sometimes a troublesome matter putting up a platform on a convenient tree, and it is often there bitterly cold; the chief point in sleeping out at night, is, as Galton points out in his Art of Travel, to get some good protection from the wind, and this is effected by any air tight partition eighteen inches high. I therefore had a bed made which was six feet long, two wide, and a boarding eighteen inches high all round; the legs six inches long to give a hold on branches or for lashings, two iron rings by each leg also affording a hold for ropes. Outside the planking, right and left, were sockets for rifles, a cloth flap over each protecting them from dew or rain, and a third socket outside the plank by the head for ammunition; this bed is just as useful as another in camp, and being easily triced up in a tree, or slung between two, it saves all trouble in muchân making.

It is, of course, difficult to get the allignment with our browned barrels at night; I have known a diamond fly sight useful for this purpose, but found the best plan to be buttoning a piece of white tape on to the ordinary fly sight then bringing it down between the two barrels, and securing it to the grip of the stock. When, however, there is any necessity for night shooting, it is better to leave the gun to do the work by the common spring gun trap, than to lie out with it. It is desirable to have a fire hole drilled in each trigger of a gun to be used for a trap; the gun is securely fastened to a couple of posts or small trees, and a string attached to the triggers is passed round a smooth stick, tied to the stock and then brought to the front, and tied to some bush or tree across the path or track which the animal is expected to pass. For hyenas, jackalls, wolves or other vermin, it is easy to place a piece of meat against the muzzle of the gun and attach the string to that.

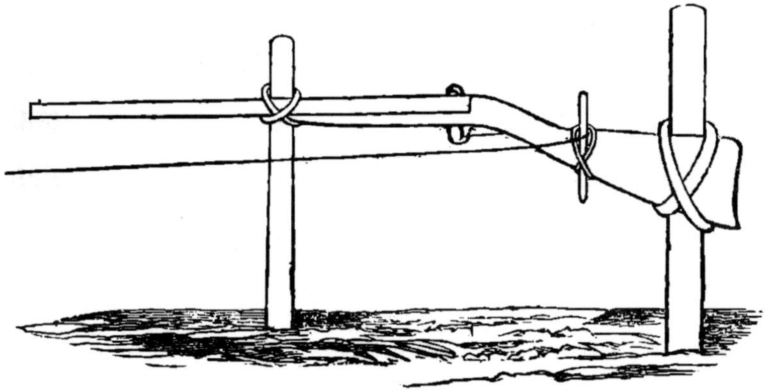

In the Doon, as elsewhere in India, if the carcase of a deer, or any other animal, is left on the ground for an hour, it is soon visited by scores of vultures. These animals are constantly wheeling far up out of sight in the sky, and they have a vision so keen that one of them is quite sure, ere long, to spy the body; and the instant he changes his apparently purposeless idle wheel in the air, for a fixed course to the object of attraction, every vulture within sight follows him, the most distant of them has others again more distant to follow him, and thus the fact of food to eat is telegraphed for hundreds of miles. On a wide plain, when no speck floats in the sky above, if a deer newly shot, be carefully covered with grass and branches of trees, and protected from jackals, it may lie till it rots for any danger it runs from vultures; but if left exposed, a few faint specks first appear in the sky, and as they increase in size, steering direct for the spot, other specks as distant and as small appear; and one after another swoop down, alighting within a few feet of their food, till, perhaps sixty or seventy of them, are fiercely tearing at the garbage. It is difficult to conceive why any one with opportunities of watching these details, should argue, as I have heard men do, that vultures are attracted by the keenness of their scent. All birds have a keen and as quick a perception when their wits are sharpened by hunger. See, for instance, five or six reflective looking, grey Calcutta crows, sitting on a house top, pensively preening their feathers, or hopping about in absolute vacancy of mind, "thinking of nothink," in fact. If at this moment perhaps a friend flies past, probably bent on business, the very flap of his wings and style of going, his general carriage, if not exactly the expression of his countenance, clearly conveying a conviction that he is going to dinner, and knows, or sees where it is to be found—how instantaneous the effect on the others, how lively their appreciation of so important a fact, and how promptly they follow the leader.

I remember, on one occasion, two European private soldiers arriving in the Doon from Meerut, where they had got a few weeks of leave, which they determined to devote in a sporting spirit, to hunting in the Doon jungles. Their weapons were not, of course, finished specimens; and as they could not afford huts and attendants, they got shelter in some cow-shed, or village out-house, bivouacking before a large fire when better accommodation could not be obtained. Firewood is plentiful enough in the forest, though hospitality is an unknown virtue among Hindoos, and though recognized among Mussulmen, is only practised towards a few of their own persuasion.

About the time of the visit of these two

privates, a tiger had been doing some mischief near the village of Suhenspore; and fired with ambition to secure such a prize, the two men went to the expense, a heavy one for them, of buying a calf worth from eight to ten rupees, and watching it by night from a tree muchân in the jungle, where the tiger was supposed to reside. While thus employed, however, the tiger killed a native in the neighbourhood, upon which the soldiers promptly disposed of their calf to the highest bidder, and appropriating the dead body, proceeded to sit over that, with a nonchalance peculiar to their class, as an inexpensive bait for the tiger. I am glad to say they succeeded in shooting one afterwards, but whether it was the same they had taken such pains to secure, I am not aware.

Every encouragement should be given to steady men, of good temper and character, to make shooting of this kind a relief to the dreary tedium of barracks.

The listless life led by our soldiers during peace in the hot weather, can hardly be conceived by residents of England. Comparatively speaking, little is done to provide interesting occupations or amusement, that indeed, which has been aptly denominated, "the unacknowledged necessary of life" for our soldiery; and if in a bracing and genial climate, excitement, to a certain extent, is necessary for the healthy action of the mind and body—how much more necessary is it in the enervating, and mortally hopeless heated stagnation of station life in the plains of India.

Efforts are sometimes made by officers in our higher class regiments, to interest and occupy their men when cantoned, by promoting national sports, and amateur theatricals; but the systematic, universal, and business-like mode of setting to work to provide amusement, which prevails in the French army, is wanting. Spasmodic gaiety subsides before the hot weather begins, and the soldier is driven to drink, in the delusive hope of escaping the effects of depressing atmosphere and maddening vacancy of mind. Government would be amply repaid in the health and happiness of its troops, and the saving of some portion of the expenses incidental to sickness, or intemperance, if it subscribed by wholesale, to every illustrated periodical published in England, as also a selection from the non-illustrated press, for six months in the year, and sent a copy of each paper to every European regiment, or depôt in India, from April to October.

At one time, not very long ago, when our political horizon was clear, and the blighting action of the hot winds and weather at work, the practice of striving for transportation by committing some crime, so slight as might ensure such relief from present misery, became very general in our Bengal army.

So soon as our soldiers found that by throwing a cap or glove at, or slightly striking some superior officer, they could hope for the punishment of transportation to Australia, they eagerly embraced the prospect of escape so afforded, and acts of insubordination and consequent courts martial, succeeded each other with startling rapidity.

The Commander-in-Chief, seeing clearly that

such a state of things must soon be subversive of all discipline, promulgated an order, intimating that the extreme penalty of military law, and not the more lenient punishment of banishment, should in future attend every instance of striking an officer.

The men, however, did not, unfortuately, believe that the threat would be carried out, and before the first instance of the offence which succeeded the notification could be tried and disposed of, some three or four had occurred.

Among other instances, was one related to to me by a friend shortly after, at the place of its occurrence. A young Assistant-Surgeon, from the neighbouring stud depôt of Haupper, had driven into Meerut, and was passing along the road to cantonments, when he met a European soldier. The man did not at all know who he was, and had, of course, no personal antipathy to him, but seeing, from the gold band round his cap, that he was an officer, he took off his own light forage cap and threw it at him. The incident was reported, and the offender, whose object was recognition and trial, was brought before a court-martial, who found him guilty and sentenced him to death, their finding was approved and confirmed in accordance with the warning duly issued by superior authority.

The young surgeon, the innocent cause of the prospective fatal termination to the affair, would gladly have averted the soldier's fate had it been practicable, but he was powerless under the peculiar circumstances of the case, while the prisoner himself never apparently dreamed of the possibility of the sentence being carried into execution.

The funeral procession of a condemned soldier takes place, so to speak, before his death, the troops are all paraded to witness the execution, and their procession marches past with arms reversed, the band playing the Dead March, while the empty coffin is followed on foot by the soldier for whom the lament is played.

folded and kneeling by his coffin, at a few paces only from the firing party of his companions, whose fusils are all discharged together that it may not be known whose was the fatal bullet that terminated his existence.

The sergeant in command of the firing party is always armed with a loaded pistol, and it is his duty to walk up to the body and ensure the immediate death of the sentenced man, if the fire of the twelve executioners is not promptly fatal.

On the present occasion, after the volley had been fired, the man was found to be untouched—the feelings of his fellows were strongly excited in his favour, and they had, as the majority of his comrades had doubtless anticipated, purposely avoided hitting him. The sergeant did not hesitate between the promptings of his private feelings and his public duty; he walked up to the kneeling figure, and placing the muzzle of the pistol to the man's head, blew out his brains.

No time is allowed to military men to

brood over the solemn spectacle of a comrade's death, and, as in the case of military burial, the last words of the funeral ritual are scarce over, when the merry notes of the returning march and the quick light step of the soldiery scare away all saddened reflections; the still pageant of the execution remained fixed but for a moment, and was then rudely broken by wheeling columns, shrill music, and the rapidly dissolving lines of gay and flaunting holiday war.

But, within a few days of the event, the dead body of the sergeant, to whose duty it fell to complete the execution, was found floating in one of the wells of the barrack lines. No music or red pageantry could wash out for him the scene in which he had such a part to play. He had wandered unnoticed, or avoided, in solitude amidst the crowded haunts of former friends, till he sought for rest and forgetfulness in the silent depths of that dark well, flying "anywhere," away from thought, and out of this world.

CHAPTER VI.

IN THE HILLS.

Starting.—Passport.—Order of the March.—Barking-deer and Gooral.—Holloway's pills as current coin.—Instance of the value of quinine.—Driving for game or "Hankwa." —Benighted on the march.—"Down the Khud."—Trapping hedges in the Hills.—Description and calls of the Hill Pheasants.—Description and calls of the Hill Partridges.

In preparing for a start from Mussouree through the Hills, it is of vital importance to your enjoyment of the trip, if not to its actual accomplishment, that you should be, as far as possible, independent of the villages along the route for food. It is usual for all travellers to take a certain stock of stores with them; but many trust to getting eggs, milk, butter, flour, and firewood on the road. Now there are many places where these cannot be got, and I should strongly recommend every sportsman to incur cheerfully the expense of the extra number of Coolees required for conveying everything of the sort for a few stages, at least. Firewood can be got almost everywhere; yet one or two spare men to convey it to particular camping grounds, where it is not found, from the last prolific locality, are desirable; a small supply of eggs, bread or biscuit and butter suffice, as the gentlemen of the party alone use them; but the carriage of flour in considerable quantity, *i. e.*, four or five days' supply for the entire party, must be calculated on, as the Coolees make it almost their only food. The simplest plan on starting, is to find out the first large village on your route, in which there is a bunya, or grain-seller, replenish all vacant space in the flour-loads at his shop, and ascertain from him the next locality *en route* where a bunya resides. The Mookias, or heads of all villages, are bound to sell you food at a profitable remuneration to themselves in theory, but in practice, as they hate strangers or travellers, are utterly apathetic to trifling casual profits, and will never part with any of their stores of food, if passive resistance can effect it; they subject you to endless trouble and quarrelling if dependant on them. Nevertheless, in case of accident or detention, causing your party to run short of supplies, or sickness among your Coolees, rendering it necessary to get means of carriage *en route*, every traveller should carry a purwanah, or general order by the civil authority of the districts through which they pass, to the villagers to assist you if requisite. The order is framed much in the style of language used in continental passports, and is sometimes quite as necessary for locomotion in the hills.

In bidding adieu to the gay station of Mussouree, after hiring Coolees, purchasing supplies, and leather-covered kiltas to load them in, disposing and weighing the several loads, which should not exceed 25 seers, or 50 lbs. for each Coolee, you fix on some grassy spot about three miles out of the station as your first camping ground. Starting, as usual, soon after daybreak, and commencing the very enjoyable course of *al fresco* breakfasts; for in fine weather, the table, or if you have none, the table-cloth, is always spread under some shady tree by a stream of water, whence the kettle is easily filled, and on the smooth stones of which the Coolees knead and moisten their flour for their very simple repasts. The kilta of sugar and tea is brought to you as soon as the bacon, eggs, &c., are ready, and for this, as also for all ammunition kiltas, it is necessary to have multiplying letter padlocks, which are quite inviolable by natives, and the keys of which you are never pestered by losing.

The advantage of thus beginning practical camping, and passing a day so near the station is, that you find out numerous little things that you have forgotten, and can send back for them to the merchant's stores in the station, prior to being finally launched on system in which to regulate your marches was to determine, after collecting information from your men and the nearest villagers, what place you will halt at next day; then direct a couple of kiltas to be prepared with all the breakfast things in it at night, to start on your being called next morning. The khitmutgar (table attendant) accompanies these two kiltas, and halts at any convenient stream about four miles from the starting-point, where he has breakfast ready by the time you reach it, or, at least, a good fire lighted under a tree, at which you can amuse yourself testing your own culinary skill. While you are at breakfast, the remainder of the Coolees and camp arrive; no tents are pitched or are needed. The Coolees lay down their loads, and rapidly prepare their single day meal; sportsmen amuse themselves bathing during the day in the stream, or shooting at a mark, or look up game in the neighbourhood; sometimes, however, starting by a circuitous route for their night camp, but leaving the usual order to the head servant to start all the Coolees at 2 P.M., so that tents are all pitched, fires lighted, and, probably, dinner ready by the time the sportsmen reach their camping-ground in the evening, where, as practised in the Doon, they talk over the adventures of the day, lament the bad shots they made, or the chances they lost for want of presence of mind; or, if successful, superintend the skinning of the deer and other animals they have killed.

The first of the mountain deer which are usually bagged after leaving the station, are the gooral, and the little red barking-deer; the latter frequents woody coverts at a low altitude. It is often found even in the Doon, and frequently gives notice of its proximity by the hoarse bark from which it gets its name. It runs quickly when disturbed, and dodges among bushes and trees; its flesh is very like hill mutton, and as it frequents easy ground, is generally shot when the sportsman is beating for kalcej, or partridges, and it should be a standing rule with every Himalayan hunter, however careless he may be about having a shot gun with him or near him when marching, never to permit his rifle to be out of his reach. An intelligent servant should be chosen as rifle-bearer, and he will soon learn to put it promptly into the sportsman's hand when game is afoot. I seldom carried my own rifle in the hills, for, though some shots are certainly lost from the delay of taking the weapon from a man who is naturally liable to loiter in a long march, or to have his wits, perhaps, wool-gathering now and then—yet many more animals would escape from the unsteadiness of the hand caused by carrying a heavy weapon far in difficult ground.

Gooral frequent the steepest grass-covered hills and test the head of the sportsman in following them, they only move about and feed at dawn, and for a short time in the evening, but can be hunted up during the day when lying in nooks and corners, or under bushes or precipitous ledges whence they fling themselves fearlessly if disturbed. They look like little grey goats, and their flesh has a very game flavour if kept for a time.

There are a number of gooral on the face of the precipitous cliffs, both east and west of Mussouree, and I have shot them about the hill of Deobun; but at each village en route it is desirable to employ a Shikaree or practised hunter to shew you the best ground, paying them well if they shew you game, but giving them only the day's hire if they do not. They always petition for powder, and the traveller must exercise his own discretion, as to how far he practises the principle of aiding them to destroy the game; but as in some cases, nothing else will elicit good information as to the exact lie of the animals, it is as well to carry a small supply of a coarser kind of powder to suit their matchlocks, for the purpose of rewarding good informants.

On the subject of purchasing good information, I may mention that all the Hill men have implicit confidence (*i. e.*, all those who have not tried them) in our drugs, and will often bring supplies of milk, or eggs, and firewood for medicine, when they are careless about their equivalent in money. An intelligent traveller, by using a little discrimination, may often do much good by administering Holloway's ointment and sometimes even his pills, or by painting now and then a case of goitre with iodine. Many of the Hill men know and appreciate the value of quinine in fever or rheumatism &c., marked by periodicity, and a good supply of it, as also of Oxley's Essence of ginger should be taken. The Coolees are very liable to cramp in the stomach, especially when near the snow marches, or where from scarceness of fuel, their cakes are insufficiently cooked.

I remember, on one occasion, having a long and fatiguing day's hunting after tahr, in which though I had managed to shoot one, which we had tracked a long way by its blood, I had bagged nothing but a Moonal pheasant which I had knocked over with a ball, and had therefore staid out later and strayed further than usual. We had gone over some bad ground and reached a considerable altitude; I was accompanied as usual by my faithful attendant Kunhaya

Sing, a clean limbed young Rajpoot, who could walk apparently for ever carrying my heavy rifle; and we had taken as guide a poor cadaverous looking Puharee who had, and by his conduct during the day deserved a high character as a hunter. As the day began closing in, and we had a long way still to go to our destined camping ground, the guide showed some anxiety about reaching camp or to some made pathway before sunset, which I at first attributed to a dread of "Bhoots," malignant spirits of forest and fell, and phases of the goddess of destruction Kali or Devee as the Hill men call her. On questioning him, however, while striding homewards, or taking springing steps down broken ground in the direction we had seen our tents from a peak, he informed me that for two years he had suffered a pain in the diaphragm, which came on with more or less severity every evening at sunset, sometimes doubling him up for an hour or two with pain and obliging him, if on the hill side and in the evening dusk, to lie benighted and benumbed till the light of the moon, or even till succeeding dawn enabled him to pick his way along the never ending precipices of the hills to his village. Almost while speaking, sunset was approaching with every promise of a black night, and the Shikaree attacked with cramp, lay down on the ground declaring the impossibility of his standing, and telling us that we must leave him where he was. It was clear we could not carry him to the tents, and could do no good by remaining with him. In the day time, it might be possible for strangers to the neighbourhood like Kunhaya or myself, by taking our bearings from conspicuous peaks, to return to the exact spot where the man was from our tents; but on a dark night, torches only illuminating for a short space around, it is impossible for a stranger, without the aid of some pathway, to retrace at night the course traversed in the day. We reluctantly pushed on to camp which we reached just after dark, not without sundry misgivings as to the position of the unfortunate Shikaree lying out cramped with pain on the jungle-covered hill in the black night, but consoled by the reflection that he had done it with impunity before, and that the leopards of the hills, unlike the tigers of the plain jungle would not pay him any further attention than a serenade. On reaching camp, I mentioned the case to a Doctor who happened to be one of a party with me, and he gave me a large packet of quinine for the man, as much as would rest on a sixpence to be taken twice a day. The Shikaree made his appearance next morning, having resumed the march as soon as the night cleared up sufficiently for a born forester to recognise his course, and on paying him for his services, I gave him the quinine with injunctions to take his doses regularly. Never returning to that neighbourhood I did not see him again; but on a future trip in another part of the hills I met a party of native travellers, who recognising me at once, applied to my servants for some of the white powder which they said had effected a wonderful cure in removing the unfortunate Shikaree's diurnal misery.

There are a number of deep gorges, thinly grown with trees and brushwood, which run into the higher hills from the Doon, and while passing along the Mussouree range before striking into the hills, it is desirable to try in these what the natives call a hankwa, *i.e.*, driving game by a line of hired beaters who commence beating from one end, while the shooters place themselves in convenient positions in ambush at the other. The common native Shikarees are the best judges of the proper beats to make, as it is quite a native system of sport, and followed principally by them, or by old invalid officers, who finding their waists expanding as their calves diminish, prefer a kind of passive to active enjoyment in their sport. I have known several surow and jurow killed by this method in the immediate neighbourhood, *i.e.*, within ten miles of Mussouree; the jurow of the lower range have not, however, such splendid antlers as their brethren the burral singhas of the ranges just under the snow. The only precaution necessary while awaiting the approach of the beaters while hânking is to maintain profound silence, and to choose your ambush to leeward of the line that the game must come, otherwise they scent and dodge you.

Marching on one occasion, in company with Lieutenant Speke of the 65th N.I., we started from a place called Munjâl for Rampore, a distance of about fifteen miles on the Sutledge river, we had fired some shots at a surow, and bagged, along the pathway, some chikor and black partridge, and straggling after these to likely patches, we were separated, my Chuprassie Kunhaya alone accompanying me. The Coolees, as usual, were scattered, two or three only of one village or caste keeping together to help each other. The descent to the Sutledge, from the heights where we had last encamped, is considerable, and the banks are in some places very precipitous. I had left the usual road and turned down a narrow pathway which, from the general bearing of the road and river, must, I knew, lead along the face of the cliffs to the town of Rampore. The length of the journey was, however, much more than I had anticipated; the day was rapidly drawing to a close, and the number of clouds above the narrow valley we were in promised a black night; but the darker it became, the longer the road seemed to grow, and our long swinging steps changed to double-quick in hopes that we might sight the lights of Rampore before the day quite closed, until at last surrounding objects grew hazy, and our steps uncertain, as stones and gravel, slipping off the pathway, sounded the depth of the abyss beside us, by crashing from rock to rock till they plunged into the Sutledge which ran foaming beneath.

We had only passed two or three of our Coolees carrying loads on the pathway, and they appeared pretty sure of being benighted, but the majority had probably gone round by the road, or were far in advance, and, possibly, in Rampore. My Chuprassie and myself were soon obliged to feel our way along the path, by resting one hand against the hill side; but in a broken and tortuous track, it is difficult enough to pick your way in daylight, and it soon became quite impossible to move, as Rampore was as far off as ever, no light even visible, while the inky darkness prevented our even seeing each other. One or two of the Coolees, with their loads, managed to creep up to where we were after it got dark, moving apparently by instinct, for I could not see my own hand when they arrived. None of the party, now amounting to five, were, however, able to advance beyond where we were, the path appeared abruptly to terminate, probably descending a few yards by rude notches cut in the rock, I attempted to grope my way down; but mistaking some inequality I found, in feeling with my foot, for a step, the support, whatever it was, gave way, and I scrambled back with difficulty. I then commenced firing my gun every minute, in hopes the sound might reach Rampore, not that any native would move hand or foot to assist us, but thinking that Speke might have reached it by the upper road before it grew dark. No sound was, however, returned, save the echoes from the opposite rocks, and the monotonous wash of the Sutledge river, and I began to contemplate the possibility of perching where we were all night like cormorants, with, perhaps, an interlude of rain to vary the cold of the night—when, suddenly, the sound of footsteps and voices, and, directly after, the flash of several pine torches, broke on us, as Speke, with three or four natives, dashed round a sharp turning in the pathway at the double, to hunt us up. We got on easily enough then to Rampore, but heard, on reaching it, that the greater number of our Coolees who were coming by the main roadway had not yet arrived. We were arranging a party to send after them, and hurrying the preparation of some refreshment for ourselves, when the sound of numerous voices outside the little stone guest house we were in, announced their arrival; but the hurried repetition of the ominous words, "down the khud" sent us quickly out to make inquiries. The khud is the term used in the hills for all deep precipices, and the term *down the khud,* as then used, might well take away the breath of those who well knew what it was to stand at the khud's edge, and gaze down its dizzy depths to where the eagles floated lazily about; and from whence, a body thown would part with life long before it reached the bottom of the abyss, a shattered mass of shapeless flesh.

The Coolees described to us, with nervous volubility, how they were coming along the upper road in the dark, one of their number being close to the wooden railing, placed to prevent accidents at the most precipitous places; an indentation of the line of the precipice brought it a little within the line of the railing. Owing to the darkness, however, this could not be seen, and, before he could stop or recover himself, the man had slipt between the rail and the roadway; he gave a cry, they said, just as he fell, and they heard the noise of the stones, &c., displaced by his fall; but, after a second or two, they could hear or see nothing, and, native like, had at once hurried away from the scene, scared by the accident, and only happy that it had not happened to be one of them. Speke and I instantly bolted into the guest house, one to light the lanthorns, and get some ropes, and spirits and water in a bottle, the other to rig out a kind of hammock with a blanket, and the ridge pole of a tent. My man, Kunhaya, got ready quickly, as pretty sure of going wherever I went; and in a few minutes we were calling for volunteers among the Coolees to come with us after the man; but our proposal was only received with an incredulous smile. Who was willing, we asked, to come and search for the man, and save him if still alive? Willing! why of course no man was willing. Volunteering did not accord with their idiosyncracies, and sympathy with a fellow creature in distress is scarcely conceivable in the Gentoo mind; our excitement on the subject was evidently considered childish; and, on our pressing the point, Speke's mate, or chief of the Coolees, enlarged with indignant eloquence on the folly of risking any more valuable lives; one man was dead and gone, and we should do nothing till the morning. Our suggestions as to how he himself might like to lie, with perhaps two broken legs all night, at the bottom of a khud, were scornfully disregarded, as quite irrelevant to the question. It was absolutely necessary, however, that we should have six men with us to carry the body if found, whether the man was dead or alive; so we adopted the Asiatic mode of simply seizing the six ablest, and intimating, that if they did not come quietly, they would have to do so *vi et armis*, and after a good thrashing. Upon this they cheerfully acquiesced in our plans, and appeared merely to have been looking out for the first specific declaration of our sentiments. Speke, however, sententiously intimated to the mate, that he would dismiss him next day.

We set out by the mid cliff path by which

I had come, and after going along it for about a mile, watching narrowly the edges of the road to mark any signs of abrasion, we soon came to a broken tea chest, a basket, and other articles, but saw no trail across the path to lead us to suppose that the man had past it. We therefore commenced climbing, adhering as closely as we could to the line of traces, made by the articles of his load which we had found. The facility with which the giddiest heights can be climbed on a dark night, with only the aid of a lanthorn, is wonderful; the light of the lanthorn only reveals the proportions of the rock and soil on which you stand, and by which you climb; all the depths, immeasurable by the eye, which produce sickness and giddiness in daylight, are enveloped in darkness. In like manner, on a very foggy day, when thick fleecy clouds have rested below the edge of a precipice, that I could scarcely stand on, and gaze from in fine weather, I have been able to traverse the entire length with a perfectly steady head and firm foot.

Our Coolees climbed like cats, and one of them came on the object of our search about half way between the upper and lower roads. He was apparently half paralysed with fright; stunned and scared by his fall, he made no answer to the questions put to him; his whole mind seemed concentrated in the idea of clinging, with cataleptic tenacity, to the ledge on which he had unconsciously effected a hold during his fall. Ignorant in the pitch darkness of his position, of the distance he had fallen, or the shape of his resting place, or any means of access to it, any movement might have been fatal; and there, if we had not come, he would have remained through the long night, or till fright and exhaustion sent him lopelessly down to the Sutledge.

We ascertained that though a good deal bruised, he had no bones broken, and after a dose of brandy and water, more for his mind than his body, we carried him to Rampore. Speke's good-nature making him forget all his threats against the mate.

Little did we then think, while congratulating ourselves on our escape from the dangers of the khud, that we stood, that same moment, on the brink of a far more dangerous precipice—that the massacres of Meerut and Delhi had already occurred, and the natives of Rampore had caught the first faint murmurs of the storm; though we, from our sojourn in the snow, were profoundly ignorant of our position; and that, within a few days, we should both be hurrying back through Rampore, on our way to the plains; myself to volunteer for service in the Doâb, and to seek to take life as ardently in the ranks of the Meerut Ressalah, as we that night had tried to save it; and Speke, poor fellow, to his last fatal climb, through a leaden rain, up the Cashmere breach at Delhi.

When the snows fall in the month of November, pheasants and other game are driven southward from the higher ranges near the watershed; the natives, therefore, taking advantage of their compulsory migration, just before the snow is expected repair long hedges, which by years of small additions they have prepared, extending to some places across hills to a distance of four or five miles in length. These hedges are made of branches cut from the woods in which they are situated, and are just sufficiently high and thick to tempt the game to save themselves the trouble of jumping or flying over, by passing through one or other of the numerous gaps purposely left in them by the makers; but in every one of these gaps there are nooses placed which are attached to the spring of a bent sapling, the size of the gap is always proportioned to the thickness of the noose string and of the sapling, which is found most conveniently situated for joining and bending into a springal. Thus a small hole which will admit nothing but a pheasant or a kakur requires but slight tackle; a gap between two trees, perhaps, which a stag might choose, can be supplied with a spring stake driven into the ground, if none of the saplings near are strong enough; and the constant worry and drag of even a small looking springal will soon wear out the strength of the strongest deer, if a firm grip by the noose is once taken; these nooses are sometimes not visited for days by the natives, and the musk deer or other animals caught, are appropriated and eaten by leopards.

The hill pheasants and other birds which are trapt in this way, are of course very perfect as regards plumage, and the English Shikaree, Mr. Wilson, prepares for sale some very beautiful sets of game birds so obtained. I observed among his testimonials, one from an ornithologist in London, who not only complimented him on the beauty of the specimens he had sent him, but also, on "the care with which they had been shot!" none of the important parts, bones, beaks, or skulls &c., had been injured, which the ornithologist evidently attributes to Mr. Wilson's skill with the arquebus. Poor indeed must be the feat of shooting a goose at five miles with the Armstrong gun, compared to the dexterity of which the cockney bird-stuffer must suppose those sportsmen possessed who can so shuffle the shot which they fire from their guns, as to dodge all important aids to "setting up," when killing an unusually fine "specimen!"

But the natives don't depend on these hedges alone for their supply of game in the winter; when the approach of the snow is gradual, *i. e.*, when not more than four or five inches of it falls in a night, the deer take warning and rapidly move down hill, to an altitude where they are safe from any heavy drifts; but if, as is sometimes the case, two or three feet of snow fall by some long continued shower, the gooral and other small deer are regularly trapt. Then their legs and small feet cause them to sink up to their bellies in the snow, and they can only progress by a laborious succession of short springs, which leave a well-marked furrow in the snow and frequently compel them to halt and take breath; but at early dawn, after such a fall, scores of villagers are on the alert, they have a kind of boot or stocking made of goat's hair, which both keeps their feet warm and prevents them slipping on the snow. They can of course often walk over snow fields in which the deer's legs sink, and if after a survey from some convenient peak they observe a deer furrow in the distance, they go to it, mark the direction in which the animal was travelling by the cast of the particles of snow displaced, and following it up are very soon able to knock the animal on the head with a hatchet, or if not, to kill it with a matchlock from a convenient range of twenty or thirty yards.

I used generally to wear the highland kilt in the hills, my entire suit being made of a grey woollen kind of cloth called Looee, which is brought from Affghanistan. I found this kilt very convenient for this snow traversing, as bare legs do not hold the wet like pantaloons, and on taking off my goat's hair boots, I had only the trouble of putting on dry shoes and stockings.

Snow hunting is very good fun, but a very poaching plan of procedure, and anyone who has witnessed it will not be surprised at the comparative scarcity of game in the finest looking game forests in the summer.

There are six different kinds of pheasants, and five of partridges to be met with in the hills, some of them are well known in England having been introduced alive with a view to their propagation in our game preserves. I give, however, a list and description that the reader may be to some extent independant and recognise the varieties when meeting them. The best plan for obtaining an accurate idea of the plumage of the different varieties, both male and female, is to purchase one of Mr. Wilson's complete sets of bird skins, which can be commissioned through Messrs. H. G. Scott and Co. of Mussouree. The sportsman should, however, also learn the cry of each variety, and their several minor calls; as when travelling through the jungle, some faint note close at hand, which the uninitiated would not notice, may arrest the steps of the practised hunter, and direct him to game which would otherwise have entirely escaped him. Himalayan sportsmen are obliged to rely much more on the keenness of their own senses than English shooters ever dream of, for although some assistance may, in the hills, be received for a time from active cocker spaniels who will flush game, yet they soon fall victims to the numerous leopards of those neighbourhoods, and often become, when not eaten, so wild as to be of very little use.

The six pheasants in the order of their rarity are, the Kaleej, Moonal, Koklass, Cheer, Hûnyâl, and Loongee. The kaleej is the commonest, and the loongee the rarest, and most difficult to secure of all Himalayan pheasants.

The kaleej, both male and female, are about the same size as the English pheasant, similar in shape, with the long tail, but they are adorned with crests. The male when young is nearly black, but gets, when older, a number of silvery white feathers over the body; the female is the ordinary brown game-mottle colour, and both have bright red skin round the eyes, characteristic, with suitable changes in colour, of all the pheasants. They have a short, sharp whistling chirp as their cry.

The koklass are nearly the same size, perhaps a trifle larger, and the female in a dress almost as quakerish as the partner of the kaleej. They are long-tailed, and the male has some rich alternations of slate-coloured and sienna hackle-like feathers on his body. Their cry is a deep note, repeating the word "kokla, kokla."

The cheer is considerably larger than the koklass; the male and female very much alike; long-tailed, russet-coated, and only differing slightly in size, the male being the larger.

The male moonal is a gorgeously plumaged bird; the head, neck, body and wings bright blue, beautifully iridescent, and covered with a gold and copper metallic lustre. The weak point in his costume is the tail, which is short, fan-like, an ugly Indian red colour, and sometimes with a patch of white feathers at the base. The female is the same shape as the male, but a very game-looking bird, with the ordinary brown mottle feathering. Their size and weight is nearly that of a turkey. When separated, or setting in trees, they give a soft, long-drawn cooing note, a cry of enquiry, either as to the position of their mate, or of suspicion of strange footsteps in the neighbourhood. When flushed, they dash down the khud like sky-rockets, uttering a loud, sharp whistle, much louder, but somewhat like the kaleej.

The loongee, or Argus, is the most beautiful of all pheasants. It derives its name from being covered with a number of bright white spots. There are two kinds; one of which has the body all red with white spots, the other, with a dark grey body, and brilliant red about the breast and head; it has also a curious bluish skin apron, pendant from below the beak, and, at certain seasons, a pair of thin round horns, about an inch and a half long. The female has a red and tan body, and the spots are of a duller shade than the male. Their cry sounds something like that of the goat, and they will sometimes commence it as if in anger when some slight noise suddenly disturbs the stillness of the forest, such as the firing of a cap, or the crack of a branch. On a like occasion, also, the kakur will sometimes begin barking. The Argus is nearly the same size as the moonal.

The hûnyâl, or snow-pheasant, is the largest of all; the male and female have the same plumage, a lightish game-mottle, with white patches; their call is very like that of the moonal, and though I fancy I could recognise the difference, I believe the real reason of our always knowing which is calling, is, that they are found at different altitudes, and on dissimilar ground.

I have, of course, mentioned merely the commonest cry of each bird, which strikes the ear of a sportsman; no doubt, a naturalist who studied their habits, spied out their private life, and listened to their domestic disagreements, might write a whole vocabulary of sounds as learnt among them.

The partridges of the Himalaya are the black, grey, chikor, pewra, and snow partridge; the black partridge, or francolin of Europe, is as beautiful a game bird as exists. Its jet black breast, and brilliant white and dark red in the wings and head, with the game mottle of its back, make it look like a cross between the black cock and red-legged partridge; the female is much duller in plumage, approaching in its feathering to the russet of the common partridge. Their call can be exactly imitated by taking a tailor's thimble (open at the ends) fastening a piece of wet parchment or bladder over one end of it, and when dry, puncturing the centre of the same with a fine hole, through which thread a horse-hair knotted at the end. If a little resin is rubbed on the horse-hair, and it is rapidly drawn with a jerking motion between the finger and thumb, the francolin's call is produced; it is only necessary to mark the time or feet used generally, viz., two long, three short, and two short. The grey partridge is so like an English one that it need not be further described.

The chikor is simply the Indian edition of

the French red-legged partridge, rather larger and brighter coloured, it has the red beak and legs, slate-coloured body, and barred wings and tail of its European cousin. The call is something like that of the common fowl, especially when half-a-dozen chikor are sitting or feeding together, though they are so like lumps of earth in appearance that they can hardly be seen, yet the querulous chirping conversation they carry on often attracts attention and discloses their position.

The pewrah is a slighter bird with a few sienna coloured feathers mingled in the russet of his game mottle, but otherwise very like our English partridge.

The snow-partridge is black with white spots all over it, larger than any but the chikor, and has a loud whistling call. It is easily recognized, being perfectly distinct from all the others, from the absence of all game feathers in its plumage.

The woodcock need not be described, being exactly the same in appearance, though lighter in weight, than our English woodcock.

CHAPTER VII.

HILL PECULIARITIES.

Polyandry.—Social Classes.—Bazgees and Dancing Girls.—Dirt and Disease.—The Plague in the Hills.—The deserted Village of Sarkot.—A Hint on Hydropathy.—The Colonization Question and Trade.

As it may be interesting for a sportsman passing through the country, to know something of customs, of which he must note the results without understanding their causes, unless he starts with some rudimentary instruction, I purpose noticing some details of polyandry, temple-worship, &c., in the Hills.

There are in the old sanscrit epic of the Mahabharata various histories, many of them, or rather much of each of them, being doubtlessly fabulous; amongst others are detailed the fortunes of the five Pandava princes, and the history of their adventure in an archery contest at the Court of Drona. The character of the reward to be given by the king to the most successful archer was unknown, but the five Pandava brothers agreed to divide the prize if any of them should prove the winner. The eldest of the brothers, Arjun, was declared victor, and received as his prize the king's daughter, Draupadi, who was doubtless considerably surprized to find that, under the agreement already made by Arjun, she was equally the property of his brothers, or, possessed five husbands instead of one. Arjun and his wife and her other four husbands, also, lived for some years at the fort of Bairath, the remains of which, or rather a Ghoorka structure on the same site, are still visible on a hill near the north-west corner of the Doon.

It is a remarkable fact that the system of polyandry thus introduced, though almost universal in the Jounsar and Bawur pargunnahs, hill districts attached to the Doon, is apparently unknown in the hills of Gurhwal and Kumaon on the east, or those of the Simla superintendency on the west.

In the Jounsar district, when the eldest brother marries, the woman is equally the wife of his younger brothers, though the children are, by courtesy(?), called the children of the eldest brother. When much difference exists in the ages of the brothers of a family, as, for instance, when there are six brothers, the elder may be grown up, while the younger are but children, the three elder then marry a wife, and when the young ones come of age they marry another, but the two wives are considered equally the wives of all six.

It is also remarkable that wherever the practice of polyandry exists, there is a striking discrepance in the proportions of the sexes among young children as well as adults; thus, in a village where I have found upwards of four hundred boys, there were only one hundred and twenty girls, yet the temptations to female infanticide, owing to expensive marriages and extravagant dowers which exist among the Rajpoots of the plains, are not found in the hills where the marriages are comparatively inexpensive, and where the wife, instead of bringing a large dowry, is usually purchased for a considerable sum from her parents. In the Gurhwal Hills, moreover, where polygamy is prevalent, there is a surplus of female children. I am not aware what effect the practice of polygamy in Turkey has on the relative members of the sexes born, but, so far as my Indian experience goes, I am inclined to give more weight to nature's adaptability to national habit, than to the possibility of infanticide being the cause of the discrepance found in Jounsar.

The great body of our Hill men are Rajpoots, there are a few villages of Brahmins, but both the one and the other are such heterodox Hindoos, that their intermarriages render the distinction between them destitute of all real difference, while some of them even keep poultry, an abomination to all but the very lowest of plains Hindoos.

These *soi-disant* Brahmins and Rajpoots, are the upper section, or gentry, of hill society, their residences are recognizable in almost every village by being superior in make, and possessing the more elevated portion of the village site; the lower range of huts, which usually form a distinct group from those of the owners of the soil, are inhabited by the Dôms, or Hâlees, who are sometimes *de facto,* though not *de jure Brittanice,* hereditary bondsmen to the Rajpoots; by bazgees, who are, both men and women, professional dancers and singers in the temples, and by the various mechanical trades, blacksmiths, carpenters, &c., whose art is of the most primitive kind. The bazgees are a numerous class, have no land of their own, and seldom cultivate. Their dancing is tame and senseless, the music hideous; but their female children form the principal portion of those devoted to the temples, or, in other words, and as in other parts of the world, devoted to the priests, and numberless holy mendicants, who wander fat, lazy, ash-covered, ochre-coloured, and insolent from one place of pilgrimage to another. These girls were largely supported in the former hill revenue settlements by government grants of rent free lands, which have now to a considerable extent been resumed; but it should not be forgotten that our government, in its ostensibly liberal minded and impartial support of the religion of the mild Hindoo, by upholding rent free tenures, and grants to Hindoo temples, is indirectly aiding something more systematically vicious than our "Social Evil."

The men of all castes in the hills, are short and of poor physique; they look worn, and get deep lines on the face at a comparatively early age. The young women are often extremely pretty; those living in the higher and colder villages, having at fifteen or sixteen, a complexion as fair as many Spaniards or Italians, and with very regular features; but they grow unaccountably darker as they grow older, and are hideous old hags, only less ugly than their plains sisters, when forty.

Strangers need not, however, except when the pathway leads through them, see anything of the dirt or disease of hill villages, which appear at a little distance, all that can be desired in picturesque beauty and apparent comfort, for where stone, wood, and slates are plentiful, the houses are naturally very substantially built. I believe that the indescribable amount of dirt and filth of these villages, does, at times, materially affect the health of the inhabitants; but it appears that it is only under certain conditions of thermometer and barometer, that disease is generated in them. It is quite possible, therefore, to point to pig-styes whence no pests are propagated.

The hills are in what are called the plague latitudes, but for a long time, the disease known to the natives as the mahamurree, or great death, was supposed by our medical men to be but a severe form of typhoid fever. It appeared during spring and autumn in the

Kumaon and Gurhwal hills, and extended on one occasion to the Rohilcund plains; but I have never met with it, or heard of it, in the hills north of Mussouree. Its advent used to be presaged by the death of domestic animals, and even rats and mice, a sign well known I hear, in Egypt, and a stricter diagnosis soon led our physicians to declare the fact, that the mahamurree was identical with Egyptian plague. As soon as the true character of the disease was recognised, our government, in 1852, appointed two doctors, both of them of the allopathic, or regular drug school, to take measures for checking the disease; their medicines proved utterly worthless, or powerless, for the cure of persons attacked; but their sanatory measures, though of a kind only possible in Asia, proved a blessing to the people, in preventing in many localities, the generation, *ab initio*, of the poison.

When these doctors received their commission, I happened to be on sick leave at Nynee Tal, in the Kumaon hills, whence access to the infected districts was easy. I felt convinced, from what I had heard of the pathology of plague, that its cure by the ordinary wet sheet packing, or hydropathic poultice, was, humanly speaking, certain and easy; and hearing that one of the medical commissioners was about to pass through Almorah, I presented myself at that place, and solicited permission to accompany him, and try my hand on some of the cases we might meet. The medico was a liberal minded, and thoroughly honest young fellow, who had already had some experience in the disease, and he at once said he should be glad of my company, and willingly allow me to try what I could do, as the administration of drugs only brought European science into contempt; medical skill was of no avail in the cure, and he had already outlined his sanatory scheme for prevention. We were bound for Gurhwal, and got on swimmingly as far as the Suneeana bungalow near Lohba, in the province of British Gurhwal, as I had received the necessary purwanah for carriage and supplies, from the Deputy Commissioner of Kumaon, and without which they could not at that time have been secured at all. The doctor had, of course, every assistance officials could give him. At Lohba, however, we were in a new district; the purwanah and government Chuprassies were for the medico alone, and after waiting for some days, I received in reply to my application for the necessary passport, a letter from the local authority, refusing me all assistance, on the ground that my irregular system would throw discredit on the plan patronised by government. This would have been more reasonable if the drug treatment had not failed already; there was no help for it, however, I could not run the risk of travelling under my friend the doctor's purwanah, far into the interior, as I should be stranded in the province, unable to proceed or return, if the termination of my leave, or any other cause separated me from my medical friend; he, moreover, was obliged to join his brother medico, whose professional views not being so liberal as his own, would not at that time be as pleasant a companion I therefore remained at Lohba, in hopes of hearing of some accessible plague village; and as soon as the two doctors were at a safe distance, some natives, who had heard of my object in visiting the district, came to inform me that plague had broken out at the village of Sarkot, about seven miles off; but they kept the fact concealed from the medicos, as no case they had attended had yet been known to recover. It is but just, however, to state, that throughout the district, I could only hear of a single traditionary case of a man recovering who had been attacked by the plague; and the native belief of its infectious and contagious character, and the entire uselessness of anything they can do for the sufferers, causes them to abandon the infected, and the villages in which they are, as soon as the distinctive symptoms of the disease are declared.

I began to find living difficult at Lohba, the local officer having acquainted the official who brought me his refusal with its contents. I found I was already known to the natives as "the gentleman who was not to have any food or Coolees." This unenviable distinction made it difficult for me to get even coarse flour to live on. If I had anticipated the difficulty I should of course have provided against it.

I, however, started for Larkot, determining to pitch my tent somewhere near it, taking a number of blankets, sheets, &c., which I had brought with me, and enjoining on the natives in the neighbourhood to report all I did, and wherever I went to the Commissioner, to prevent any misunderstanding with the local officer or medicos. A severe murrain had visited Gurhwal that season, and not only the neighbourhood of the villages, but numerous places along the pathway were in a pestiferous state from the dead bodies of cattle lying about. In the jungle, on my way to Sarkot, I met the pudhân, or head-man, who had fled with the rest. He informed me that plague had appeared in his village for three years successively; he had lost his wife the year before, but had married another. This year, six cases had occurred ere they fled; four bodies had been buried, a fifth lay in one of the houses, keeping a grim watch over the deserted tenements, and the sixth (a brother of the pudhân himself) was supposed to be still living, having been then only three days ill.

I proposed that he should accompany me and attend on his brother, but I could not argue him out of the fright which custom and bad example had engendered. "Dustoor" or custom, is an all-powerful argument with a native. He said, "Sahib, in this illness, the son abandons his father, the parent his child, and the husband his wife; my wife and children have fled with me, and, were I to be hanged for the refusal, I would not touch my brother." My sweeper, however, a man of the Meehter, or lowest caste, from the plains, who had never seen mahamurree, agreed to assist me for five rupees in "packing," &c., and I next day got all necessary appliances taken to a stream by Sarkot, making a native carry one of the string frames on which their goats sleep during the rains, to the same spot, which, though filthily dirty, was the only bed procurable. The pudhân had agreed to go with me to the stream if not compelled to enter the village, and to call to his brother to come out if living, on condition that I would not hold or detain him (the pudhân) when the brother appeared.

Sarkot contained, apparently, about fifty houses and one hundred cow-sheds, mixed together as usual; no living creature was visible, but I did not go through the village, the air being poisoned by the bodies of cattle dead from murrain.

At first, no response was made to the pudhân's screams for his brother, and the former said he thought he might have got the "Bhêm," or horror, a delirious paroxysm, and got into the jungle. He said that his brother, whose name was Jowharoo, had, on the second day, managed to light a fire in a shed near, but the owner had driven him out with stones for fear of his infecting it, and put out the fire.

Suddenly, however, several of the villagers who had come with us, commenced moving off, and the pudhân, as he retreated, pointed towards the village to a bush behind which, on going up, I found the unfortunate Jowharoo—a miserable wretch, who seemed scared at the approach of his fellow-men, while the dirt and lines marked by tears on his face, told a long story of lonely misery.

His pulse was ninety-six ; a good deal of low fever, and a swelling on the neck. The wet sheet packing reduced his pulse within the hour twenty-six beats per minute, and care and treatment for two days assured him that he would soon be well. I then heard that the two medicos had returned to Lohba, *en route* for Chuprakote. I, therefore, rode over to report progress, and challenge them to come and judge for themselves. They had, however, heard of numerous cases at a place called Bounghar, and, after giving me some interesting details of their experience, left me for that place, while I returned to my tent by Sarkot.

Jowharoo soon became quite well, but no one in the village would touch him till he had been on a pilgrimage to Budrinath, and been purified by the Brahmins there. I had been procuring necessaries by purchase with difficulty from the people of the place, and as his brother promised to hire Coolees for me to get back to the Kumaon province, I made over my blankets to my patient, and returned. I heard, afterwards, that a commission of French physicians, in a report on quarantine, had declared that the only satisfactory cases of cure of Egyptian plague that they had met with, had been treated hydropathically.

Now, the principles and practice of this system are so generally known, that if any traveller be ignorant of it, he can acquire all necessary acquaintance in a week. I know by experience that native attendants can be taught the packing operation in half-an-hour, so that, although any sportsman, hearing of mahamurree, may avoid its locality should he think it advisable, yet I believe there is no sufficient cause for abandoning any good shooting ground on its appearance.

As regards the question of the possibility

of Anglo-Saxon colonization in the Himalaya, I am aware that the matter has temporarily lost importance, owing to the good understanding we have been cultivating with the great Indian feudatories, and the security we have purchased by some concession of English doctrinaire principles to Asiatic facts; but a consideration of the practicability of the question may not be without interest.

I have myself been over the greater part of our Hills—the only part of which I have no local experience being the grass lands of Cashmere—but I believe that the most practical opinion that can be obtained on the question is that of Mr. Wilson, known in his own part of the world under his *nom de plume* of the "Mountaineer," from his contributions to the "Calcutta Sporting Review." He is well described in Colonel Markham's book on Shooting in the Himalaya. He originally went to India as a trooper in the 3rd Dragoons, was inoculated with a taste for the sport of the Himalaya during a visit on sick leave to Landour, and yearning after his return to Yorkshire, for the far-off region under the snowy peaks, he worked his way out to Calcutta, and travelled up on foot to the scene of his present mountain home, not far from the source of the Ganges, at a village he received from the late Rajah of Teeree, where he has resided for many years. His knowledge of the natives, of the country, and of the means of procuring an existence, or an independance, is, of course, perfect; and I feel convinced, both from communication received from him, and from my own experience, that colonization, in the ordinary acceptance of the term, is impossible.

The physical character of the country is a bar to ordinary agricultural pursuits, on any but the scanty scale already monopolised by natives, and no mere labourer could compete against their prices. No doubt a system of military settlement, the localization of a corps of European Riflemen with their wives and children might be effected by liberal Government assistance; but its success in a pecuniary point of view, whether with reference to the men themselves, or their masters, would be problematical. There is, however, an endless field for English enterprize in the cultivation of tea, and in trade with Thibet and Central Asia. The slopes of the Himalaya afford space for sufficient tea to supply all Europe as well as India, and the returns at present on the investment of capital in its cultivation are upwards of a hundred per cent, with a demand that must remain for many years practically unlimited.

I speak of borax and wool in a later chapter; I believe, however, that an article of infinitely greater importance has, up to this present time, been strangely neglected. Almost every animal that lives in Hundês, except the domestic sheep, is covered during winter with a downy wool called pushum by the Hindustanees, which is of exquisite fineness, far surpassing in quality, though not in length of staple, any of the wools of Europe. It is obtained most plentifully from the shawl goat, and largely used in the famous shawl looms of Cashmere; but the dogs and wolves of Thibet, the ovis ammon and even the yak are all more or less possessed of this pushum wool. At present it only passes from the wool marts of the Indus banks in Thibet to Cashmere, where a portion is appropriately used in shawls, and a good deal wasted in the thick soft material known to Cashmeerees as pushmeena. Should a demand for it arise, the numberless native traders of these snow valleys could contract for large quantities from Gartok and Daba; and the best test of its being able to bear the expense of goat, jooboo, and sheep carriage over the ghâts is, that common sheep's wool bears that expense at present. Pushum is an article at present almost unknown in England, and her Majesty's civil and military officers are prohibited, under pain of dismissal, from entering into agricultural or commercial speculations in the country; but I believe that any Anglo-Saxon trader who will bring energy and capital to commence the traffic in Pushum wools from Thibet through our hills, and also to ensure a manufacture retaining their distinctive character to sight as well as touch, will rival, in the novelty and importance of the fabrics he will found, the far famed alpacca looms of Saltaire.

CHAPTER VIII.

SOME HILL EXPERIENCES.

Tea planting and manufacture at Gwaldung.—Kill Kakur and Jurow.—Sand flies.—Kill a Kustoora.—Jungle of gigantic Box-wood.—Kill a Baloo and catch a Tahr.—Poisonous honey, and Procession of drunken Coolees.—Marching in the rains.—Leopards and Dogs.—Leeches.

THE Provinces of Kumaon and Gurhwal are admirably adapted for the growth of tea, and the abruptness of the hill sides renders it possible for European planters to have their houses at the elevation of six or seven thousand feet, where they have an English temperature, and are yet within easy reach of their plantations which should not be brought above five thousand feet.

There is a large quantity of unoccupied

land available for tea cultivation in Gurhwal and Kumaon, and the terms on which it is allotted for that purpose by Government are extremely favourable. At a place called the forest of Gwaldung in Gurhwal, I came on a location which had been taken by a young Englishman for tea planting; the Government tea garden of Ayartoli was within a day's march, and the garden of Paoree about two or three on the other side. He had adopted the very sensible plan of consulting some of the Chinese manufacturers at the Government garden, as to what they thought the best site for a plantation, and as the Chinese are energetic sportsmen, wandering long distances in search of game, they mentioned Gwaldung as one of the most promising locations they had seen (I recommend this plan of choosing a site to intending emigrants). He then got the Deputy Commissioner's permission to erect boundary pillars at the points he had chosen for the purpose; and as no village lands approached his location, there was no difficulty in the matter. In accordance with the Government regulation in force on the subject for these two provinces, all barren or jungle land within the area which was unfit for the growth of tea he got free, as also all the tea lands for four years, after which time, the latter are subject to a rent of one anna, or a penny halfpenny, per acre per annum for the first year, two annas for the second, three annas for the third, and so on ; but the Government has bound itself never to take more than sixteen annas, or two shillings per acre for the lands, and as it takes twenty years holding to reach that maximum, while all the rest of the location is held free so long as the rent for the cultivable area is paid, the cost of land, is, as compared with the profits of tea planting, very trifling.

It is necessary, where the slope of the hill side is very abrupt, to terrace all cultivated land—a succession of low stone walls, like a gigantic flight of steps, affording narrow level strips of earth for fields, and if any unusually heavy rain carries away the earth from an upper field, it is only carried down to the next, not lost in the nearest ravine. A large extent of this terraced land is lying uncultivated in most villages, and might be taken from the owners on long leases, at from three to four annas per annum. Tea plants and seed to any amount available from the nearest Government gardens are allowed gratis to planters; the tea plant takes four years to obtain a sufficient height for plucking, and then produces, on an average, eighty to one hundred and sixty pounds of manufactured tea per acre, for which from three to four shillings a pound is obtained at present on the spot, which sufficiently accounts for little or none of it having ever reached England.

Labourers are easily procured at four rupees, or eight shillings, per mensem, and Hindustani tea-toasters who have learnt the manufacture from Chinamen imported by Government, at from one pound to one pound ten per mensem. This accounts for the fact that all the tea planters are at present making from two to three hundred per cent on the capital they have invested, and that any planter who can devote his own energies as well as two or three thousand pounds to the trade, may safely count on two or three thousand a year for the next fifteen years at least; for the limit of the demand for India could hardly be reached in that time, to say nothing of the facilities of transit to Europe which railroads will soon afford. At sixpence a pound, tea planting and manufacture would pay, and it is not, by any contingency now conceivable, likely to fall below two shillings in ten, or one shilling in twenty years.

The busy time in tea making is from April to September, during which months there is always something to be done in the tea manufacture, and packing of the spring and autumn picking; thus the planter can easily have five months holiday in the year, from October to March, if he leaves a trusty foreman out during the first named period have all a burnished look, which they lose if left for a few weeks unpicked; these are the only leaves fit for tea making, the full grown ones affording an infusion little better than hay. So that a tree which has just been picked, looks at first glance just as full and bushy as ever. As the picking begins in the fourth year of the plant's growth when about two to three feet high, the removal of the young buds and shoots in picking, keeps the whole plantation at that height.

There are, of course, various gradations of quality, between the youngest and best leaves, and the full grown useless ones; but all are picked together, and brought in the same baskets to the roasting sheds, where a portion is given to black tea makers and a portion to green ditto. The black tea is curled by toasting in iron basins, and when completely dried, the different character of the leaves composing it become conspicuous; there are four sorts of black picked out in

India, the coarsest and badly curled leaves are first separated, chiefly by sifting, and form the commonest kind of black tea, or "bohea," the other three kinds are separated chiefly by hand picking, viz: pouchong, souchong, and fine souchong. The leaves allotted for green tea require more manipulation than the other, are rolled and curled a good deal by rubbing with the hand on the working table, and when all the sap is removed from them, are separated into gunpowder, (the best), young hyson, and hyson skin.

The difference in the colour of the black and green trees, is sometimes developed by the portions used for black being kept rather longer before toasting than the leaves for green tea; but a great deal depends on the manipulation used by the manufacturers while the leaves are in the toasting pans, as they can turn a basket of leaves gathered from one place, and dried at the same time, half into black and half into green tea.

The slight frosts which appear in winter

time at an elevation of five thousand feet in the Himalaya do not injure the tea plant, and it is not liable to the blights, or alternations of good and bad seasons, which affect indigo, sugar, and opium.

The various plants, by the flowers and leaves of which the scenting of tea is effected in China, have been introduced into our Indian plantations, but I have never known of their being used for the purpose. Government is, very properly, anxious that the tea sent from its manufacturies should be perfectly pure, and objects to allow even of the adulteration of scenting. When private speculators enter more into the trade, they will doubtless supply the public with whatever they buy with most avidity, like the Chinese, who do not hesitate to dress some of their green teas with prussian blue and gypsum, though expressing considerable surprise at the barbarous taste of their customers in prefering such a mixture.

As my friend had merely pitched his tent on an open grass knoll by a piece of water in the forest, and commenced building a bungalow, sowing tea, and burning wood simultaneously, he had visits from jurow and other deer almost daily. His native valet, having a taste for sport, brought him some pheasants while I was there, having borrowed his master's gun to kill them with; and on my going into the neighbouring jungle I shot a kakur within two hundred yards of the location, and a fine specimen of the jurow about the size of a galloway a little further on. These animals are generally found at a moderate elevation, like that of Gwaldung, which is five thousand feet, because they there find the character of forest and food which they most affect.

In descending from Gwaldung to the Pindnee river, we were persecuted by a small species of fly, which, though scarcely perceptible, so minute are its proportions, yet creates considerable irritation by its bite, and leaves a black spot of congealed blood under the skin; they only make their appearance in warm valleys, and though their tattooing is scarce visible on a black skin, they give a curious piquancy to a European's face and hands, and a bold and expressive character, both by swelling and spotting, to the nose.

At Ramnee, four marches north of Gwaldung, I came on a good shooting ground for moonal pheasants, and musk deer—shooting one of the latter. The hair of the musk deer, like that of most of the deer tribe which live in the snow, is composed of grey and white tubes, which are extremely brittle, but each hair being so large that the hollow is distinctly seen when one is broken off. This provision of nature enables these animals to lie out on the surface of snow while freezing, without losing animal heat, or suffering from the numbing influence of their bed, as they would do but for the natural air cushion which their thick coat of tubings interpose; while close to the skin they have the downy coating of pushum wool. The musk bag, or pod as it is technically termed, is only possessed by the male; it is about the size of an egg, and situated under the skin, between the orifice of the urethra and testes. When cut open, the musk looks like rhubarb pills, and sometimes has small pieces of dry grass mixed with it, though it is difficult to conceive how the grass gets there. The pod usually contains from one to two ounces in weight, and is worth thirty shillings per ounce, being used as the basis of many of our English perfumes; but as the animals shed their musk at certain seasons, the pod is sometimes found almost empty. Mr. Wilson informed me that he and his Shikarees, one season, killed a hundred and fifty musk deer.

Beyond Ramnee, at a place called Sem Khurruck, I came on a wood or jungle of box-wood trees, which I commend to the attention of the two London Illustrated Papers, or any persons having large wood engravings to get up. The trees were as tall as firs in England, and some of them as thick round as a man's body; the wood is known as pâbur lukeree by the natives, and may at present be cut without let or hindrance, in any quantity, by anyone who wants it; the only use the natives appear to put it to, is in making hair combs. There is, I know, another place in the Himalaya, where a similar growth of box trees is found, and blocks of sixty pounds weight, or a load for a man, would cost merely the cutting and carriage down to the Ganges, if commissioned for engraving purposes, through any one acquainted with the localities.

There are some fine sambah, or jurow deer, at the lake of Eranee, five miles beyond Sem Khurruck, and several black bears. When out looking for koklass pheasants, with a village Shikaree, named Deopooree, at a hill above Kowar, I came across a young bear which I bagged, and some of the men caught a young tahr, which I reared for some time by letting it suck a goat, but it died of rain and long marches afterwards. The native attendant who caught the tahr was a long and anything but handsome Coolee, who grew a kind of shaggy stuff like a yak's tail on his head, but came to complain indignantly against the kind and quality of the supplies furnished at the village we stayed at—saying that, among other deficiencies, his hair was being utterly ruined for want of oil.

When crossing the Bireh Gunga stream, between the Goodyar Tâl, and the village of Elanee, some of my men pointed out to me a large honeycomb attached to an overhanging rock, about one hundred feet above us, which, like a roof, completely sheltered it, and made it quite inaccessible. The villagers told me that a sahib had fired a rifle ball at it the former year, but it only made a small hole, bringing down a few drops of honey. I saw at once, that by striking the surface of the rock just in front of the comb, my heavy rifle ball would be flattened out like a sheet of paper, and cut it off the rock, I therefore fired both barrels at the spot. Down came the greater part of the comb with a perfect stream of honey, and a cloud of infuriated bees; we all fled instantly, the Coolees throwing down their loads and seeking refuge in the jungle, while a herd of goats coming down the opposite bank was scattered in all directions; a low howl now and then from the dogs in charge, testifying that the bees had discovered that their noses at least were not covered with hair. Rolling a blanket round the entire body is a complete protection, as the sting is not long enough to reach through it, and as the Coolees all carry blankets, very few of them, comparatively speaking, got stung. As soon as the bees commenced swarming again on the remnants of comb left sticking to the rock, the natives pronounced all danger passed, and rushed forward to secure some of the honey. The villagers of the neighbourhood seized on large pieces of the comb, which they said was a powerful medicine for cattle; but my Coolees, who knew nothing about the kind of honey they were collecting, secured as much of the liquid portion as they could find, and ate it. I merely tasted some, as it had got mostly mixed with grass and gravel; but I observed that the few bees lying about, were of a much larger and heavier kind than any I had seen before, and the honey soon began to have dismal effects on the Coolees, who staggered about as if intoxicated. We had ascended a narrow path with precipitous ground on one side; most of the Coolees who had eaten the honey had abandoned their loads at the bottom of the hill, but they had sense enough left to know that if they staggered about as they were doing much longer, they would go over the khud. So the first of them gravely went down on all fours, the rest following his example, and amidst shouts of laughter from their unaffected companions, this solemn procession of drunken Coolees wound its way uphill, affording those who had failed in the scramble for honey, and therefore did not grow sick, an opportunity of discanting on the evils of gluttony. The villagers then favoured us with the information that the honey was of a poisonous kind, which they only used as medicine.

During my last visit to Thibet, where I had intended to stay until the rains were over in the hills, I got so tired of living entirely alone without any European companion to speak to or practice English with, that I determined, though the rains were in full force, to start away from the snow and to push through the rains to Mússouree. I had some curiosity to ascertain what such an experience would be like, and whether it was possible to travel or not at that season. I found that the practicability or otherwise of keeping one's health on such a journey, depended on the possibility of securing a dry shed of some sort to dry your traps and sleep in. As the rain came down in torrents almost all day and night, it was of course impossible to keep dry at all from the time of starting after breakfast for the march, up to arrival at the village intended for the halt; and it was equally impossible to pitch your tent or sleep in its reeking folds if pitched. No native, whatever your discomforts or difficulties, would give you shelter, unless he mistook you for one of the district officials, so the only plan was to walk straight into any uninhabited shed or shelter you could find, and proceed to light a fire for your followers, of course paying liberally for any firewood or other notice that the apathetic inhabitants vouchsafed you, which, however, they never dreamed of, unless it was ordered in an authoritative tone. I made a point of paying one rupee, or two shillings for the night for any place I occupied, and though that would for a villager have sufficed for a year's rent, I believe the owners would prefer, even if guaranteed such terms, to prohibit travelling and exclude strangers. A sick man arriving at a native village would, if none of his own caste were in it, be allowed to die under any tree he lay by, without a chance of assistance from its apathetic inhabitants.

Throughout my hunting tours I have not seen above half a dozen leopards in the jungle; they conceal themselves so carefully, that even where plentiful and doing serious damage to dogs and goats, and often caught in traps, they cannot be sighted for shooting.

While marching along one day through the rain, followed by my dog-keeper who was leading a large Thibetian puppy, called Pluto, a slight scuffle and a cry from the dog made me turn round just in time to see a leopard, which had sprang at Pluto from the thick grass by the pathway, rush down the khud. The brute had evidently been following us for some time for an opportunity of appropriating the dog, but failed in his spring. In no wise daunted, however, it coolly returned to the bank just above us, and running along parrallel to our course, was gazing in hungry admiration at the proportions of Pluto, when a ball in the stomach from my revolver, drove it from the contemplation of more digestible diet.

An officer living in the hills told me, that a friend of his had sent him a favourite greyhound bitch to pass the hot weather under medical certificate in a cool climate; and his sweeper was on one occasion leading her backwards and forwards on the gravel walk in front of the house, and he himself was looking on when a leopard sprang from some bushes in the neighbourhood, and though failing to seize the dog as it sprang behind the keeper, yet managed to leave a scratch on the flank which showed a very narrow escape for the little animal, who, nevertheless, uttered no sound of surprise or dread, apparently nerved to silence by the greatness of the danger; but no sooner was it taken into the house and saw the door safely shut, than it indulged itself, in reward for the restraint it had practised, by setting up a prolonged howling for some minutes—in fact giving way to violent hysterics in ludicrous caricature of superior organizations more sensitive than sensible

On the first appearance and fall of the regular rains, the grass or jungle throughout the hills swarms with small leeches, which when you march in any costume but the kilt, wander up your trowsers, down your stockings, and gorge themselves to overflowing with blood before you suspect their arrival. Their bite is scarce perceptible, but the irritation which it brings on afterwards is often very troublesome, and they have a strange fancy for fixing in the nostrils of dogs, causing a tickling which makes them continually rub their noses with their paws; and living in safe retirement in their narrow retreat, until, in some unguarded moment, the dog's master manages to seize the tail which they hang at times out of the nostril with a pair of pincers, and either applies a dose of salt to loosen their hold, or pulls them out at the cost of a loud yelp from the poor pointer or spaniel who has been their victim.

CHAPTER IX.

IN THE SNOW RANGES.

Rarity of the Bunchowr or Wild Yâk.—The course of the Dhowlna river. — Gold washing. — Gin drinking. — The Yong river route and its difficulties.—Coolee carriage changed for Jooboos.—Surjoo the Shikaree.—Compact with the new Coolees.—Passage of the Chor Hoti Ghât.

HAVING, prior to 1858, killed at different times all the ordinary varieties of Himalayan game, I was very anxious to employ a portion of a six months' leave, which I obtained after the Mutinies, in securing the rarer kinds of Thibetian animals, more especially the bunchowr or wild yâk and the nyan or ovis ammon. Major Alexander Cunningham, of the Bengal Engineers, speaks of the bunchowr as follows, in his Physical, Statistical, and Historical Account of Ladak and the surrounding countries, published by Allen and Co. in 1854, page 197.

"The wild yâk, brong or dong is said to inhabit the grassy plains on the upper courses of the Sutlej and Sangpo.

"The people generally believe in their existence, but I could neither procure any of their horns, nor find any person who had actually seen the living animal. Vigne was informed that the wild yâk was to be found to the north and east of Garo, that is the district of Gnári.

"As the tame yâk has been domesticated from time immemorial, the existence of wild herds in the same country may, perhaps, be doubted; but the general prevalenee of the belief is worthy of being recorded."

Now the tame yâk, known as the chowr gai, is a noble looking animal, if compared with the common bull of India; but the size of the bunchowr may be judged from the native expression that "the liver of a wild yâk is a load for a tame one."

I determined, therefore, to hunt for wild yâk in the snow valleys "by the upper courses of the Sutledge," between the Himalaya and the Kailas or Gangree range.

In pursuance of this plan, I arrived in the Dhowlna valley, in the Gurhwal district, which trends up to the Niti Pass, and several more dangerous paths across the snow, on the 17th June 1858, with the view of penetrating into Thibet. I had previously crossed the Borenda Pass into the Buspa valley, and visited Kanawur, returning viâ Rampoor and the valley of the Sutledge, at the point where it forces its way through the Himalaya. I think an account of the later journey will best describe the pleasures and perils of travelling in that part of the world, and point out the best districts by far for Thibetian game.

The snow valleys may be supposed to commence from the town of Joshimuth situated at the junction of the Vishnoo Gunga and Dhowlna streams. From thence, along the left bank of the Dhowlna, a pathway in some places precipitous, brought us by a march of about ten miles to Tuppobun, and the next day we encamped at a small guest-house, a low-roofed hut of about twelve feet square at Summunghenta. This place is sufficiently far up the snow valleys to be protected to some extent from the periodical rains, which though falling heavily a little farther south, had not crossed the higher hills, or found their way along the snow streams to the so called snow villages. During the height of the rains, however, clouds find their way up all these valleys to the foot of the ghâts, and rain, in the form of Scotch mist, is frequent though not constant.

There is a stream entering the Dhowlna at Summunghenta which issues from a snow valley, apparently not yet explored, it is called "the gorge of smoke" or "vapour;" its physical features are "fudged" in the portrait of it which we find in our maps, and the natives in the neighbourhood say that they have never gone through it, as there is no practicable path, that it contains nothing, and trends nowhere ! The stream which issues from it, however, is very impetuous and effects a natural quartz crushing of the rocks in its channel, and several Dhunias, or gold washers, visit it annually to extract gold from the sands of the bed. They use a primitive looking but neatly made cradle of reed work, and are quite ignorant of the use of mercury for extracting the gold. The Dhunias belong to the lowest caste in the Hills, and I should say from their general appearance and tenue, that gold seeking as practised by them is not a very profitable profession.

Two days' march took us from Summunghenta to Malari, the principal village of the Dhowlna valley ; during the journey, we crossed the river several times by bridges, composed simply of two or three long pine trees thrown across the stream, and with small pieces of wood tied across them as a roadway. These bridges, besides being at times at a height of thirty or forty feet, above a stream that no animal could stem or swim in, used to sway about with the weight of every one who crossed. I found it therefore impossible for a ghoont or Tartar pony, which I had intended to take to the ghât, to go any further; but it would be easy by slight repairs of the bridges and pathway to take poneys up the valley, and over the Niti Pass into Thibet. The goats, sheep and cattle used for carrying merchandise by our Bhotia traders go over these bridges with marvellous dexterity.

Intoxication prevails to an extraordinary extent among the Bhotias; they distil a kind of whisky, some of which is of full proof strength. The cost of this spirit is little or nothing, as they make it for themselves, free of all excise restrictions—so dram drinking begins every evening about six o'clock, and is more universal than in any part of Scotland. I had put up at the Punchayut Gurh, or town-hall of the place, a dirty looking building, or rather hut, but with some curiously carved portals and eaves, and on sending for the pudhân of the village at about 8 P.M., I was told that it was too late to see any men of the place on business that night, as, by that time, all were drunk! Some of the regular topers appeared to be systematically intoxicated every night, and in a chronic state of obfuscation all day, while the temperance section only got drunk on highdays and holidays! The women appeared to take no share in these orgies, it was manifestly considered by public opinion to be no part of "woman's mission" to imitate their lords in everything. All field labour, however, such as it is, in altitudes where but little can grow, is performed by the softer sex, while the husbands are absent on trading journeys into Thibet; and at home, the males appear to have no permanent occupation but spinning, which they accomplish while idling about the Punchayut Gurh, having a roll of prepared wool round the waist, from which they attach a few fibres to the hook on a piece of wood passed, at right angles, through the centre of a wooden cross, which they spin by a twist of the finger and thumb.

Now, as my object was to visit, in the first instance, the valleys about Shelshel and

Kyungrung, (which, being out of the ordinary tracks of the Bhotia traders to Thibet, are therefore the more likely, from their unbroken solitude of years, to be visited by the bun-chowr bulls, which are said to wander from mountains far away in the interior of Tartary), it will be evident from a glance at the map, that apparently the easiest route would be along the bed of the Yong river from Malari, and on this subject I have a few words to say. The map shows that near the Niti ghât, which is just south of the great Thibetian marts of Gartok and Daba, the line of eternal snow, through which our difficult and dangerous ghâts into Thibet pass, takes a bend southward, leaving the watershed line which is our boundary, and along which the snow ridge line, (except in this instance), extends; and although all the highest of the Himalayan peaks are found on spurs south of the watershed, yet the line of watershed itself is throughout so elevated, as to place a tax of difficulties, almost prohibitive, on the bulky and low priced staples which alone, up to the present time, our commerce has commenced interchanging with Central Asia, China, and Thibet. It was this difficulty which induced Lord Dalhousie, when at Simla, to direct the commencement of the great Thibet road, which takes advantage of the passage cut through the Himalaya by the Sutledge, to make a commercial artery between Central Asia and Hindoostan; but the interminable and easy gradients of that road will require, to make it worthy the design of the projector, an amount of outlay which our Government can hardly, in the present state of our finance, afford. The sums even necessary for proper repairs on what has been accomplished, appear now to be obtained with difficulty—and, until railways cover the Punjaub, the point where this road debouches on the plains must be deemed inconvenient as regards the further journey towards Europe of commercial staples from Thibet. Of the great value and importance of the Thibet Trunk road, however, and the advantages it will give us in introducing our manufactures direct to Central Asia, (instead of hearing, as we have done, of Manchester piece-goods being procurable only from Russian traders), there can be no doubt, and it is much to be regretted that the present stagnation in its progress exists.

To return, however, to the point on the map to which I have alluded, the triangular tract of land enclosed between the high snow range and the watershed line is now an uninhabited waste; it is above the range of tree vegetation excepting just at Yong, where birch trees and a kind of cypress are plentiful, but is covered with excellent grass, and an innumerable number of flowering plants; vetch, and lupins, wild onions, leeks, rhubarb, and atees (the fashionable substitute for quinine) grow in quantities.

The character of the slopes, and the entire geological formation, is more that of the table land of Thibet than of our precipitous hills, and there are throughout it numbers of small lakes, or rather ponds, which, being supplied with water warmer than the atmosphere around, form agreeable baths throughout the summer.

The names marked in the map, Rimkim, Shelshel, Hoti, Leptel, &c., are those of camping grounds only—halting places for the numerous droves of goats, jooboos, oxen, &c., which traders take for pack carrying through the tract in the summer. The height of the numerous points on the watershed, where paths from the tract enter Thibet, is not much above the table lands bordering the Sutledge; but the Yong river, collecting as its affluents all the streams of Hoti and Leptel bursts through the line of snow hills, and thus forms what would be the gate of Thibet, if advantage could be taken of the cutting made by the Yong river.

It is already easy to go from the south as far as the junction of the Girtee stream with the Yong, and from the north to the junction of the Leptel stream with that of Yong; but the intermediate portion is so precipitous that no human foot has yet traversed it, and although blasting and birch wood platforms might perhaps accomplish the narrow ledge, which serves as a road in those regions, the banks being in some places precipitous to a great height, the frequent slips of rocks and earth, or snow avalanches, would always endanger it. If, however, there are no sudden falls in the bed, and none are known or visible, all the aforesaid engineering difficulties will doubtless be overcome, whenever our trade with Central Asia grows sufficiently extensive, and the now almost unknown tract about Hoti and Leptel, would then become an important entrepot of commerce.

When I reached Malari, I sent for a resident of the village of Gumsali, by name Surjoo, who was supposed to be a great authority on all sporting subjects, and by his advice moved on next day to Bompa, the next village to Gumsali, and only a short distance from Niti, which is the last inhabited spot south of the passes.

It is here necessary to dismiss the Coolees who have come from lower ranges, and employ a number of the jooboos, a mule between the tame yâk and the common cattle, together with their owners, one native managing and loading two jooboos; also four or five extra men, who were habituated to work in a rarified atmosphere, for carrying guns, or for contingencies from sickness or accidents.

I paid up the former troop of Coolees, and gave them half a month's wages in excess, with which they appeared greatly pleased, and invested the amount in Tartar salt, which they could dispose of in their own neighbourhood for one hundred per cent profit. A present of a couple of sheep, or goats, and a a little tobacco now and then to the troop of Coolees, does much towards keeping them in a good humour.

I at first intrusted the new arrangements required to Surjoo, but soon found him out to be a double distilled scoundrel. He wasted four days on frivolous excuses, pretending the impossibility of getting baggage animals, but really increasing his demands for his own remuneration. As the waste of time made my departure more urgent, I at last applied to two men of Bompa, named Dhun Sing and Buchoo, both of whom I can recommend as active, able, and willing assistants; they got me twelve attendants, with nine jooboos and two oxen. My Chuprassie Kunhaya and a plains Bheesty determined to accompany me, though warned by the recusant Surjoo of the frightful tortures which they were to suffer from cold and rarified air.

After the preliminaries were all arranged, several packages of my things, and two servants being left at Bompa, and prompt supplies of flour, &c., being promised by the pudhân whenever my jooboos should come from Thibet for them—a further delay of one day was occasioned by the celebration of an important festival at Gumsali, at which every inhabitant with any pretensions to respectability was bound to be drunk, for which a large amount of extra strong whiskey had been prepared, where the lords of creation, from the townships of Niti, Pharka, Bompa, and Malari were all to be present, and where, in fact, it would be a sin to be sober after seven o'clock.

I could not, of course, offend the religious sentiments of my followers, by remonstrances against the performance of so serious a ceremony. We have taught the natives that the best plan for getting their own way, is to have a religious prejudice for everything they like to do, and a religious prejudice against everything they don't like to do; these prejudices have, therefore, increased greatly since the time of Menù.

My men were collected next day, and would doubtless have appreciated the present of a few dozen of soda water, had that beverage been procurable in the neighbourhood. I moved the camp in the evening to Tamersen, at the extreme limit of tree vegetation, and on the ascent towards the Chor Hoti Pass into the tract of country already described. Mr. Surjoo, the guide, who had formerly monopolized the profits of cicerone to the few English who had entered the valley, seeing me able to do without him, now came and offered to accompany me on moderate terms, but I would have nothing more to say to him. We next day reached Kala Jubbur, the last practicable halting place before crossing the ghât, passing several herds of burrul on the march, which were, however, too wild for a comparative tyro in work at such altitudes to stalk. We were obliged to carry up to the halting ground, from a lower altitude, the roots and stalks of a kind of scrubby bush for fuel. The plains of Thibet being above the altitude of tree vegetation, the only fuel used is this scrub jungle, the bushes of which in most places are kept down to about six inches in height by the wind.

I may here mention the contract made with my new employés; the men were to get four annas (sixpence) each per diem, and a similar amount was to be allowed to the owners for each jooboo; those who were employed as shikarees, *i. e.*, hunters, or rather guides, were also to have their food supplied them, and receive baksheesh, or reward, in proportion to the amount of game they showed me. This was more than natives of the labouring class usually receive; but the time of these men was valuable, as they were employed during the trading season, and would lose at least one trading trip to Thibet. All the inhabitants of our snow valleys trade; they reside from March until November in the villages just under the ghâts, where a scanty cultivation is carried on by their women, and whence they take flour, rice, sugar, cotton, &c. &c., into Thibet, bringing back borax, salt, and wool.

Most of them have some member of their families residing at Daba, or Gyanee, on the Nunakhar Lake in Thibet, to collect the amount of merchandise they require in small instalments; but from the month of November to March, the cold and snow make all the inhabitants of our valleys abandon their residences in them, and they live along the banks of the Aluknunda about Kurnpryag, Nundpryag, &c., whence they effect their exchanges with the plain beoparees, or traders, at Nujeebabad.

The means of transport they use are the chowr gai or yâk, which carries a load of from 150 to 200 lbs. and is purchased for from ten to fifteen rupees, but which dies if taken down to the lower ranges, (this animal has lately been acclimated in France). The jooboo, a mule between the yâk and hill breed of cattle, which carries from 100 to 150 lbs. weight, is purchasable for from twenty to thirty rupees, and can go without injury down to Nujeebabad in the cold weather. Lastly, goats and sheep, which cost from two to three rupees each, carry from 10 to 15 lbs. weight, and do not comparatively suffer from change of climate.

The yâks and jooboos are all bred in Bussahir, whence they are brought for sale; the goats and sheep come from the Chumba district.

We had a severe day's work before us when leaving Kala Jubbur, the next practicable halting-ground being at Rimkim, about twelve miles off, but on the other side of the ghât. We therefore started at daylight, at once leaving all traces of vegetation, and mounting ever upwards over dreary tracks of worn grey stone, and stretches of snow; some slight signs of a foot-track worn here and there on the stones being the only perceptible pathway, while among the Titanic rocks above us, a few faint patches of dim unearthly blue, like the ghosts of old peaks past away, declared our approach to the region of glaciers.

The most critical places in such ascents are generally the transits over sloping snow-drifts in clefts, or torrent beds. The snow at a slope of about 45 degrees, stretches high above the line of march on the one hand, and down to unknown depths on the other. The leader of the party goes in advance with a hatchet, and cuts out with two blows a place in the snow for his foot, and stepping on to the niche so made, he cuts another a step in advance, and so on for perhaps forty or fifty yards; all who follow, including the Coolees with loads, when there are any, follow step by step on the same spots. Of course, a false step must be fatal, but you have the additional danger that the cohesion of the snow may not be sufficient for the small patch on which your foot is placed to support your weight, when, of course, you must go down the incline, and, probably, be lost to sight for ever. An incline of which you cannot see the termination, or which ends in an abrupt precipice, or a hole in the frozen surface of a hill river, must be carefully traversed. There is only one difficult incline on the Chor Hoti, and even that is of limited extent. I have passed some requiring good nerve on the Borenda, before it had opened for regular traffic, and I have heard of a gentleman losing one of his Coolees, whose footing gave way on a snow incline. The officer and party, by a long circuit, were able to get to the bottom of the slope, which they found to enter the frozen bed of a stream; the Coolee had, doubtless, lost all consciousness, if not life, before reaching the bottom, and had been carried under the ice, through which, at a short distance from the hole, they could see the man's body, but could not get at it, nor, indeed, would it have been of any use doing so.

As we approached the summit of the Pass, which has an elevation of 18,300 feet above the level of the sea, *i. e.*, 2,600 feet higher than Mont Blanc, one of the jooboo drivers who came from another part of the country, became prostrated from want of air, or from his exertions in climbing and driving with a pack on his back, and in so rarified an atmosphere; but none of the rest of the party experienced any unpleasant sensations.

At such an altitude, snow-storms and driving sleet may be expected at any time of the year; and the sky, which had been very clear when we left Kala Jubbur, grew dark and clouded, with mist wreaths shrouding some of the peaks as we approached the top of the Pass. Just before the closing the passes, snow-storms are heavy and dangerous; scarcely a year passes without sundry losses in the lives of traders, who attempt the transit late in the season. The cold at such times is so intense, and the snow so blinding and bewildering from the entire obliteration of any trace of roadway—that if a convoy be caught in a storm, men, jooboos, goats and sheep all alike perish, buried in the snow.

My men pointed out to me several melancholy vestiges of such misfortunes in the clothes of the lost traders, which were always spread out by the spot where they fell, the bodies themselves being burned on the first opening of the passes the next season. A chequered woollen plaid, a blanket, and some other remnants of cloth, were recognised as those of the brother of one of the men with me, who had perished two years before.

An abrupt descent had to be effected for a distance of five or six hundred yards from the summit of the pass on the north side, this portion is always covered with snow, and the practicability of the descent depends on the peculiar condition of this snow at the time. If it be too soft, the yâks, &c., sink helplessly into it, and removing their packs and dragging the things down piecemeal becomes a heart-breaking labour; but when the snow is hard, or the surface frozen, it would be certain destruction for men or animals to venture on it. On our testing the snow, it was pronounced too soft, the yâks plunged into it but struggled out again. I had gone on in advance, followed at a short distance by my Shikaree Kunhaya; but a fine driving snow commenced falling, and on looking back I found that we were not followed by the rest. I had some difficulty in climbing back to find out the cause of delay, and found all the Coolees sitting helplessly on the stones above the snow drift, the greater number of them cowed by the cold and snow, and some of them fairly whimpering and comforting their companions with the assurance that we should all die. They had, with thorough native apathy, given up all attempt at exertion, and had I been a member of the Aborigines Protection Society, I might have sat down and wept sympathetically till we lost our noses, fingers, and toes; but being deficient in sweet sentimentality, and deeming their defection and collapse not only inappropriate and inconvenient, but unwarranted by the circumstances, their living in the snow regions enabling them to stand cold better than myself, I determined that it only remained for me to commence a promiscuous assault and battery on the party, laying my "alpen stock" indiscriminately on the heads and shoulders of those nearest to me. This unexpected misfortune obliterated for the time being the memory of their other woes, and they became paralytically active in undoing packs, forcing the jooboos into the drift and carrying down articles themselves, in which, to avoid invidious distinction I joined. Wet, cold and exertion fairly entitled some of us to become, as we did, rather livid, and we disposed of two bottles of spirits brought for the occasion, in striking harmony and entire forgetfulness of all caste, distinctions and prejudices. I believe that spirits are, as a general rule, unmixedly mischievous to a sportsman; but I am bound to confess, that on the present exceptional occasion, we found our dram drinking of material benefit, and as the remainder of the descent was comparatively easy, the men were soon in high good-humour, and we got along cheerily, arriving just before dark at Rimkim.

Now, in this instance, the dram drinking was strictly, what it is often falsely assumed to be, medicinal, the importance of the momentary stimulant being deemed worth the cost of after depression, or a few days' irritability of system. I have myself no prejudices in favour of either teetotal or temperance doctrines, but I have left off entirely the use of beer, wine or spirits, without however pledging myself on the subject—simply because I have found them inevitably and unmistakeably mischievous. I attribute the steadiness of my hand in rifle shooting, very much to my not drinking wine or beer, and I have never in my life known any case of a hunter giving a fair trial to the system of drinking water, who did not find he could do better in walking, shooting and endurance of every kind than when on the "strengthening system of beer and spirituous tonics." Even in the present exceptional instance, I found that those accustomed to "drink" were the first to suffer from the collapsing effects of extreme cold on the circulation, were the least benefitted by the stimulant, and soonest lost the slight fillip of abnormal or excited strength it gave.

At the foot of the dip, we found numberless traces of the bones, packs and merchandize of some droves of goats lost in former years, which were peeping through the snow. All the traders appear to have a superstitious dislike to having anything to do with the merchandize thus stranded on the ghât; they say that certain misfortune would attend any except the immediate heirs of the deceased owners who appropriated the things, and as most of the family may have perished with their cattle, and probably came from villages a long way off (the property being rather out of the reach of the administrator general) wool, borax, salt and packings lie bleaching among the bones of their bearers, till too much deteriorated to be worth removal. The difficulty we experienced in crossing the Chor Hoti was, it must be remembered, partly exceptional and due to the unfavourable state of the weather; but this Pass may be avoided altogether by those who do not mind losing a few days and going round by the Niti ghât, which is only sixteen thousand feet high.

CHAPTER X.

BEYOND THE SNOWS.

Tartars prohibit further progress.—Their Tea.—Facts regarding infusion of tea.—Hoti and Leptel.—Sight the Kyang, and shoot a Pheea.—Fossil beds at Takoolee.—Tartar taxes.—Sight the Ovis ammon.—Hunt and kill the Burrul. —Visit Shelshel.—Dispatch an envoy to the Zumpun.—Enter the Salkh Nullah and sight the Bunchowr.—A night on the Hill, and march to Kyungrung.—Thibet Geology.

We had now arrived at a quarter which, although belongiug to the British, under the watershed rule, is claimed and treated as their own by the Hunnias or Snow-men, because beyond the principal line of passes; and on the next day's march to Takoolee Shêm, I was met by five Tartar zemindars, who, having heard that an Englishman was coming over the Chor Hoti into Thibet, had, as compelled by the Chinese authorities, come to try and make me go back. They had no weapons with them but their tattoos, small Tartar ponies, and were loaded with a multiplicity of coverings and impedimenta, most of which were connected with their tea-drinking. When we reached them, they were busy cooking tea, a ceremony they go through four or five times a day, and they requested that, as a particular favour to them, if not a peremptory necessity, we should at once encamp where they were, as they had something to say to me, and we must talk together next morning. I consented to camp as they requested, though it would have been wiser to move on, as every requisition of the kind is tentative as to how you are to be managed, and every concession made, gives them the right to further demands.

Hundês affords a promising market for the coarser kinds of tea produced in our Himalayan manufactories. All the Hunnias drink tea, it is brought from China packed in lumps, which are composed of the coarsest leaves, twigs, seeds, &c., of the tea, pressed by weights into lumps, and sometimes rendered more adhesive by a slight admixture of the serum of sheep's blood; the leaves are badly dried and sometimes partly decomposed, the lumps look like tobacco, and it is called brick tea. I purchased a piece weighing four pounds for fourteen shillings, which was the market rate.

The Hunnias travel enormous distances living on nothing but tea, and what the Hindustanees call suttoo, which is the flour of parched gram, or chicken vetch. The tea is, however, prepared in a peculiar manner, they boil the leaves for some hours, or, if camping, for perhaps all night, in a small earthen vessel; they then pour the black infusion into a large copper vessel of hot water, and mix it with salt and ghee (clarified butter), adding some suttoo if they have any. This, of course, produces a species of tea-soup, and they can live for months, and undergo great fatigue in travelling without any other sustenance. I have since seen this scientifically accounted for, in the well known and interesting work called the "Chemistry of Common Life," by Johnston. He says at page 174, "that tea leaves possess as much gluten as beans and pease, but it is wasted by our system of preparation." The comparative chemical analysis of tea leaves and beans is as follows, the usual market samples being taken.

	Tea	Beans.
Water	5	14
Starch, gum, &c. . .	27	48
Gluten	20 to 25 .	24
Fat	3	2
Tannic Acid . . .	15	0
Husk, or woody fibre	20	10
Ash	5	2
	100	100

So that not only does the tannic acid, or theine, prevent, or rather diminish waste of the animal tissues, but the gluten, &c., enables reparation.

Dr. Johnston says, "There is a large proportion of gluten in tea which is not dissolved by the water in which we infuse it. It has been recommended that as an improved method of infusing tea, we should put a pinch of soda into the water along with it. The effect of this would be that a portion at least of the gluten would be dissolved, and the beverage, in consequence, made more nutritious. The method of preparing the brick tea adopted among the Mongols and other Tartar tribes, is believed to extract the greater part of the nutriment from the leaf, they rub the tea to fine powder, boil it with the alkaline steppe water, to which salt and fat have been added, and pour off the decoction from the sediment. Of this liquid they drink from twenty to forty cups a day, mixing it first with milk and butter, and a little roasted meal. But even without meal, and mixed only with a little milk, they can subsist on it for weeks in succession."

Next morning, after the Hunnias had delayed, as long as practicable, the important communication which they had to make to me, our palaver commenced, two of my trader servants acting as interpreters, the sum total of their talk proved to be—that it was impossible I should go on any further—that travelling in their country was strictly prohibited—that the zemindars, or Tartar residents of the country had no objection to my coming, but they would be fined by the Chinese authorities if I persevered. I replied, that neither they or the Chinese had any right to close that country to harmless travellers, who did not offend against their customs or laws—that if they merely rested their prohibition on the rule of might is right, or *sic volo sic jabeo,* the English would be saved a world of trouble by accepting that position, thrashing them out of their country, and forbidding them to return. That we would be delighted to see them on our side of the passes, give them every facility for travelling which our own subjects had, and expected some reciprocity. Finally, that the territory we were then on was, by the watershed rule, within the boundaries of the British dominions, and if either party were intruding it was certainly theirs; but it was quite useless arguing with them, as they had no influence over the Zumpun of Daba, the Chinese chief of the district, who was also, though to a less extent, dependant on the will and pleasure of the Garkoon of Gartok, his superior officer. I therefore picked up my rifle and walked off, telling my men to march, and the Hunnias that I should be happy to see them at the next halting ground, but had no more time to lose at present. I had, however, spent some time in exhibiting my own tea-things, weapons, clothes, and some curiosities in the shape of stereoscopic slides, beads, necklaces, &c., which I had brought as presents, and to barter for flour, &c., if procurable; they therefore saddled up and cantered along after us, two of them keeping watch over me wherever I went in search for game.

I past several beds of shell fossils on the road, and noticed a number of ponds of clear spring water, the temperature of which was warmer than the atmosphere, and in which I would have bathed, but for the bitter cold of the wind, which would have been anything but pleasant while dressing. I saw on the plain for the first time, a few kyang or wild horses, also a number of pheea, a kind of marmot, and some burrul. The marmots are in appearance exactly like the prairie dogs of America; they never stray far from their burrows while travellers are in sight, and quickly alarm any of their kind who may not be on the alert, by a shrill whistling noise which sounds something like "pheea," the Hunnia name for them. They sit often erect on their haunches, like rabbits, and one which I shot with my rifle, turned so quickly into his hole, that I had to dig the body out from a depth of about four feet.

At Takoolee Shêm, I found two extensive beds of lias formation, the surface reduced to soil, or rendered extremely friable by exposure to frost and air, while the melting of snow and rain had, by removing the surface soil, left exposed over one bed, a large number of ammonites, and over the other a singular looking crop of bellemnites. I found in the first bed in the space of an hour, some twenty or thirty very fine specimens, varying in size from a pin's point to a yard in diameter, the interior often beautifully crystallized, and glittering with iron pyrites; on breaking a number of large black boulder looking stones, I frequently found the nucleus of the lump to be an ammonite, or some other fossil neatly nestled in the centre.

These ammonites are much prized by the pilgrims to Budrinath and Kylas, to which places they are sometimes taken by traders; they value especially those which have been worn round by the action of some stream, just retaining the waving nautilus like lines of the fossil; they are known as sulgrams, or more correctly salik rams, by the Hindoos, who in the plains suppose that they are procured by perseveringly praying on the bank of some river in the mountains, (everything very wonderful has its locality in some mountain or island, according to the *savans* of the plains) and the sulgram comes swimming along the surface of the water to the holy devotee.

I went out a while at Takoolee, after ovis ammon, of which, though rare in that quarter, I recognised three with the aid of my binocular glass, near the summit of a neighbouring hill. Scaling the precipices of the Hoti and Leptel tracks where I then was, was easy work compared to the danger of shooting on the Thar grounds of our own hills, as the country approaches the character of the Thibetian table lands, rather than that of our precipitous hills, excepting merely on the faces looking to the pathless crags and glaciers, which overhang the passage through the snow chain of the Yong river.

The Hunnias with us did a little business on our return visit to Takoolee, which it will be more convenient to note here, in collecting the transit dues from some Rajpoot traders, who were encamped at Takoolee, and were about to take their wool, borax, &c., across the ghât; the Chinese government gives little or no pay to its officers, but they have great advantages in their trading operations, as they are entitled to tax everything coming to, or leaving the country, and are to some extent exempt themselves. Long custom and extensive trade, as also the vital importance of the grain trade to the Hunnias themselves, has established prescriptive tables of tolls which limits their exactions.

One of the traders, a fine stalwart looking man, was introduced to me as a great shikaree, and having fraternized on the subject of Thibetian game, he agreed to go out with me the next day, and show me some herds of burrul. We started at daylight, accompanied by two of my men, and making over a small hill to the south, went along the slopes by the Yong below Rimkim; these slopes are crossed in several places by small streams, running from glacier beds to the Yong, and one or two of them had to be forded. In the largest, our legs to the knee were exposed to the stream for about two or three minutes, and though our circulation was very good from the exercise of walking just before we entered, yet the intense cold of the water caused firstly sharp pains in the legs, then discolorations, which even showed clearly through the black skins of my companions. I then felt the sensation of numberless needles and pins running into the legs, as when they "go to sleep," from arrested circulation, and in a few minutes, had we not got on terra firma again, and restored animation by friction, I believe we should have suffered from partial frost-bite.

From the extreme caution and manœuvring of my guide, I gained a clearer idea of the extraordinary powers of scent possessed by almost all the game animals of the snow, than I had before possessed. Sound, sight, and scent are the positive, comparative, and superlative dangers against which the sportsman must take precautions, and strain his faculties to screen from his game when stalking. Burrul, in that locality, and ovis ammon will take alarm at the taint of human beings in the air at two or three miles off, if the wind be favourable, or blowing gently towards them. There were several herds of burrul at intervals of one or two miles apart on the slopes, though owing to their similarity to the large grey stones lying about, they were quite invisible at that distance. My guide recognized the first herd at about one mile, and sunk at once with his face to the grass, all of us doing the same, and lying motionless until we had clearly determined to what direction the flock was feeding. We then drew carefully back to the shelter of a small ridge behind us, which led to a stream hard by, where we could head them.

We spied over the crest of the bank to watch the course they were taking; those behind soon finished the little grass left by those preceding them, and would then step on in advance a few paces, the herd thus continually advancing in one direction, till two or three of the leaders lay down, and the rest of the herd followed their example. We had no means of approaching in their present position, and as they might, on rising, alter their direction, we had to lay quiet for about half-an-hour, when they resumed grazing on the same line as before. My guide finally placed me in an admirable position, up to which the herd came trotting, as if they had instinctively acquired a feeling of restlessness and danger, and I threw away the opportunity by two execrably bad shots, which secured nothing, and naturally disgusted the guide. We, however, went through the same performance further on with another herd, and after one bad shot, I fired recklessly into the herd at about six hundred yards off, and happening to strike a young burrul with a raking fore and aft shot, rolled it over dead. The men, having had nothing to eat that morning, at once cut it up, and lighting a fire of the roots and stalks of the creeping and scrub bushes about, threw a number of slices on it to cook. We then all sat round on our haunches, and strict etiquette on the occasion required, that when any of us descried a piece of flesh sufficiently frizzled, we raked it out of the ashes, rubbed it between the palms of the hands till all superfluous charcoal, wood-ash, or gravel was removed, and proceeded to chew the morsel while hooking out another.

The flesh, for reasons already explained in Chapter V, was perfectly tender, and after washing our hands and faces in the nearest stream, we sent a man back with the burrul gralloched, to lighten the load, and proceeded to stalk another herd. My experience, on this occasion, should be a warning against using sharp elongated conicals for shooting; the shock produced by a round-headed ball is incomparably greater than that caused by the needle-like points used for Jacob's projectiles. On a former occasion, I shot a gooral through the chest, the sharp-pointed ball entering behind one shoulder, and passing out at the other; but so slight was the shock, though the wound was a fatal one, that, after springing from the ground once, the animal quietly trotted off through bad ground for upwards of a mile, and I got it afterwards by a chance shot breaking one of its legs.

On the present occasion, we had stalked a

large herd to within seventy yards. I rested the end of my rifle on a piece of stone in front of me as I knelt down to fire, and singling out two burrul feeding together and so placed that one ball would pass through both of them, I fired. Both burrul sprang up clear of the ground, as the gooral had done when struck in the same way; and as the body of the herd broke away to the left of us, I noted two burrul leading off in another direction, which, I felt quite certain, were mortally wounded. They, however, went too far for us to follow, as it was growing late, and the guide, who knew nothing of the scientific reasons for their escape, was in a state of speechless disgust at what he considered my bad shooting. I never loaded afterwards for game without cutting off first the sharp ends of my bullets, and would recommend every sportsman, having a needle-pointed mould, to have a brass or iron moveable cup fitted to it for casting bullets for game-shooting. We returned to our tents pretty well tired out by the day's work.

On the next day's march to Shelshel, while walking along without any expectation of seeing game, we suddenly came on a large Thibetian wolf, or chanko, which, however, escaped us. The rifle was comfortably cased in its leather cover, and though ready to follow up any head of game suited for stalking, was not at hand for such unexpected apparitions as a chanko on the foot-path. I shot some snow pigeons which were very like, though rather lighter than our common wood-pigeon. We camped close to the watershed line at Shelshel, as I determined to devote a day or two to the Salkh nullah and its environs, which, being utterly uninhabited tracts without any trading lines crossing them, were sometimes unvisited by human beings for years, and, therefore, favourite resorts of the bunchowr bulls from the Kailan range.

Great excitement prevailed among the Tartar escort with us. New Tartars and ponies arriving while others were starting off with expresses for the Zumpun of Daba; the Bhoteea zemindars were urgent that I should make some compact with them as to the time of my stay, and the places I was to visit, that they might send it off to the Zumpun as a proof of their zeal and diplomatic ability. I, therefore, told them that I had come to hunt for game, that my present intention was to shoot about Tazang Kyungrung, Chounglas, and the nullahs of Salkh, Leptel, and Keo, where I would probably remain about a month; but being anxious to avoid all chance of getting the zemindars into trouble, and having some curiosity to see the Zumpun of Daba, I dispatched one of my Coolees as an ambassador to that potentate. My envoy was instructed to present a brilliant Victoria tartan cashmere plaid to the Zumpun, to solicit an interview for me, and to intimate that I had brought a stereoscope, with sundry photographic pictures and other presents, which I should be happy to present to him at Daba in person. The Coolee, having duly gone through a course of stereoscopic examination, and instruction in the principles of photography, was sent off with but hazy views on the subject of the science, though fully prepared to elaborate a description of the wonders he had seen, which would be much more marvellous than the reality. I was aware that the Hunnias being, to some extent, connoisseurs in woollens, would admire both the material and colouring of the plaid.

On the 5th of July, I started from my tent at Shelshel for the Salkh nullah, taking nothing but some food and tea for the four men with me and myself, and a number of blankets. I had little hope of coming across wild yâk the first day, and our party was moving up the gorges of the Salkh stream without having any videttes thrown forward, when suddenly, as if by electric shock, the whole party threw themselves on their faces, and I saw, about five hundred yards a-head, six magnificent bunchowr bulls, all as usual jet black. Their eyes and noses were unfortunately all turned towards us, and it was evident they had long been expecting us, and put on the *qui vive* by the scent. Though I crawled out of sight on all fours, and ran up as far as I could behind cover, I could not get within certain striking distance of their heads or hearts; and being under the delusion that they would not move off more than a few miles if not alarmed by firing, I let them pursue their stately march, up the snow gorge they were entering, without a shot, leaving them to be followed next day. As it was too late to go far, we continued our course for the camping ground, sending a vidette about five hundred yards in advance, who, however, was soon signed back; for we saw a mile in front of us, amidst a chaos of mighty rocks, a conical hill with a flat top, on which, motionless as his mighty pedestal, stood a gigantic solitary bull gazing grandly on the wastes around him, sole living monarch of the solitude—but looking at the distance, whence we saw him, like some majestic monument of iron. This monster's head and hide I have now among my trophies at home; but it took many days of hard work to obtain them. On my hurrying forward, stumbling over bad ground and snow, as fast as the essential necessities of retaining both stalking screen and the leeward side would permit, I found the grand pedestal empty; and, on ascending it cautiously, saw the big bull frowning defiance at me from a peak at least three miles off. My guide declared his belief that the first herd we had seen were off to the Leptel nullah two marches away, and that the big solitary bull was making for Keo which was three days' journey; his first conjecture was wrong, the second proved right, we therefore returned to the side of the Salkh stream, where being without tents, and at an elevation where it freezes every night in the year, we commenced building a low wall of stones to keep off the wind, and get up sufficient fire to warm some water for tea. While so employed, the guide seized my hand, and pointing to a rocky ridge far above us, showed me against a clear sky the sharp outlines of the herd of six bulls we had seen in the morning, who appeared to be standing stupified by the insolence of our intrusion.

This, however, was the last look they had at us, or we at them, they started for fresh diggings during the night, and though hunting in that neighbourhood for a fortnight I never came across them again. We found the night as a matter of course bitterly cold, and when I awoke in the morning, my top blanket was covered with hoar frost, and a cup of tea by my side, frozen hard.

The whole of the next day we saw nothing, and in the evening moved to Kyungrung to which place I had directed the camp left at Shelshel to proceed.

I staid for several days in the Kyungrung nullah, finding numerous traces of yâk, but seeing none. There is a conical hill at the head of this valley called the Jelmowr Hill, and the stone of which it is composed, is supposed by the natives to have valuable medicinal qualities. I collected a number of pieces on the spot, a curious soapy looking stone with numerous green shadings through it, and containing apparently a good deal of

The geological strata on this side of the passes are like those of the greater portion of the Himalaya, principally the oldest sienites and schists ; there are, however, numerous volcanic rocks about Kyungrung and Kuntchego. Trap, basalt, surpentine, and amygdaloid, being plentiful. The Hunnias find numerous fossil bones in the boulder table land just north of the Himalaya, the strata appears to be, and I have heard that the fossils also are, much the same as those of our Sewalik just south of them. The fossils are called "Bijlee Har" (lightning bone) by the natives, aerolites are very common about the passes, and I picked up several myself which the natives called "Devee Gola," (the bullets of the Goddess Devee).

CHAPTER XI.

IN THIBET.

Short of Supplies.—Chinese Officials and their Policy.—The Robbers of Hundês.—Commercial Staples and means of Transport.—Humnia modes of War.—Kill the Kyang, Nyan, Hunyal and Chasa on the Plains of Heemachul.—Interview with the Zumpun.—March to the Keo Nullah.—Kill the Bunchowr.—Return to Bompa.—Parting advice.

THE difficulty of crossing the Chor Hoti during bad weather, of course renders Englishmen in Thibet liable to dearth of provender, when their jooboos are detained, or their hunting unsuccessful. A dispatch of three jooboos and their attendants, which I expected with supplies from Bompa having been delayed by snow for three days, and I having omitted the precaution of ordering a dispatch through the Niti ghât, we found ourselves on short commons. The only game with which I had lately been able to come to close quarters, were some unfortunate burrul, that had fallen from precipices coated with ice in the winter, and which were of course unfit for food, though pretty well preserved in the snow; their fate, however, proves, that not only accidents happen in the best regulated families in a highly civilised and artificial state, but they are inseparable also from a state of nature.

There are some kinds of wild vegetables procurable about Hoti and Leptel which are an agreeable addition to a dinner table, which may perchance consist of nothing but the flesh which the sportsman obtains in hunting, and the flour he brings over the passes. I give the local names, as they are not to be found, I fancy, in any written dictionary, and it might be difficult to obtain the articles by description.

The wild onion	Jumboo
The wild leek	Dûmm

Red Rhubarb	Tatree
Green Rhubarb	Dodloo

All of these are but dwarfish varieties, yet possess a good deal of generic flavour; there are a number of wild gooseberries, currants and raspberries at lower altitudes in our snow valleys—the two former crude and uneatable, the last well developed and palateable.

I sent off some men to purchase food from the residents of a grazing station two marches off, called Dungpoo. I had seen plenty of game through my glass at long distances, and would have killed numbers of burrul at Kyungrung, if I could have commenced work with the experience about sound, sight, and scent, which I afterwards acquired; but though stalking with what a sportsman in the plains or lower Himalaya would deem useless care and caution, I drove all the game in the neighbourhood wild. My messenger returned from Dungpoo without being able to effect any purchases, they said the people were very willing to sell, but did not dare to offend the Chinese authorities. I however made my men buy some young shawl goats; tame yâk's tails, &c., from some traders who were passing, and as my supplies came over the ghât soon afterwards, we were independent. I had requested the Coolee whom I sent to the Zumpun, to embrace the opportunity of buying in Daba some brick tea, tame yâk tails, and turquoise; he returned to Kyungrung with all those things, and answered that the Zumpun was from home, but that his wife had appropriated the plaid which she greatly admired, and guaranteed that her lord should meet me at Surkya when I reached that place. All nations and creeds, excepting Europeans, are free to trade in Hundês—Ghoorkas, Hindustanis, Sikhs and Willayutees, may all travel to Gartok or elsewhere; but though the people of the country are friendly towards us, the authorities prohibit our entrance, forbid our receiving food or supplies of any kind from the people, and though unable altogether to exclude Englishmen, revenge themselves by sometimes fining the inhabitants of the district through which they pass. My Hunnia guard informed me that two English sahibs had, a few seasons before, crossed through the Byans Pass to the Munsarâwar Lake, and gone sailing about on it in a leather boat (probably mackintosh) which they had brought with them ; the Hunnias were all in a condition of gaping and speechless surprize at their impudence : the Garkoon evidently considered that the dignity of the lake had been insulted, he fined the Zumpun of Daba 200 rupees, and afterwards sent for him to Gartok to answer to the charge of permitting such a flagrant offence to take place in his district, as the Zumpun did not return, I presume he was dismissed.

The Zumpun is District officer or Sous-prefet of the valley of the Sutledge. The present incumbent is supposed to be more intelligent than the generality, and will probably hold office for more than the usual term of three years. He appears to have almost absolute authority over the people of his district; he comes from a distant part of the Empire, the province of Bood, has no income allowed him, but what he can make by trade fines, &c., of which the major portion must be paid to higher authority in revenue, and has only about a dozen police, and an unpaid writer styled vizier, as establishment. He can, however, call out any number of the inhabitants of his district for military or other duty; they have a great dread of him, and he in turn has a profound respect for the Garkoon or Commissioner of Gartok his immediate superior. The Garkoon's establishment is not on a much more splendid scale than that of the Zumpun; he has under him for executive duties, a sort of captain of police styled Surpoon, who commands one hundred men, ragamuffin soldiers armed with ill-made matchlocks, and two, sometimes three swords a piece; this last awe-inspiring arrangement is intended to make them a match for the robbers of Hundês, who are at times very numerous, appearing and disappearing again mysteriously, like land quails, or influenza, and who come to the attack after discharging their fire-arms with a sword in each hand, and one tied round the waist.

The superior officer to the Garkoon is a species of Lieutenant-Governor, styled " Shib-chid" who resides about a month's march from Gartok, in the province of Bood ; this accounts for all the district officials, all belonging to a clique from that province.

My men told me that the Zumpun himself, when travelling, had been robbed by the Dacoits of Hundês ; and that, in winter, when all our snow valley villages are abandoned, they have been known to cross the Niti ghât and plunder the empty snow villages. They have an almost superstitious dread of English fire-arms, and ascribe unlimited powers to them. On one occasion, my guide, Dhun Sing, said he and a number of Jowaree traders were attacked just over the passes, on the Thibet side, by a band of Dacoits ; they did not kill any of them, as the trouble was quite unnecessary, the traders did not think of resisting, and their goats with the merchandise on them were all driven into one large herd, and appropriated by the Dacoits, while the traders passed the night after their loss in bemoaning their having to start for their homes next morning destitute of their property; but, early next day, a young Englishman, with two Shikarees, arrived on a hunting expedition, and so afraid were the Dacoits of his gun, that they absconded at once, abandoning the plunder; and the only difficulty the traders, had was in separating their respective droves. They took care, Dhun Sing said, to leave the place next day with the Sahib, who was going back to Millum.

All the inhabitants of our snow valleys trade; they reside from March till November in the village just under the Ghâts, where a scanty cultivation is carried on by their women, and whence they take grain, flour, rice, sugar, cotton, &c., into Thibet, bringing back borax, salt, and wool. Most of them have some member of their families residing at Daba or Gyanee, on the Nuna Khar Lake, to collect the amount of merchandise they require from the Hunnias, and from November to March the inhabitants of all these valleys abandon their villages and live along the banks of the Aluknunda about Kurnpryag, Nundpyrag, &c., whence they effect their exchanges with the plains Beoparees at Nujeebabad. The means of transport used are the chowr gai, or tame yâk, which carries a load of from one hundred and fifty to two hundred pounds, and is purchased for from twelve to fifteen rupees, but which dies if taken down to the lower ranges, (the acclimatization of this animal has since been effected in France). The jooboo, or mule, between the yâk and the hill breed of cattle, which carries from one hundred to one hundréd and fifty pounds weight, is purchasable for from twenty to thirty rupees, and can go without injury down to Nujeebabad in the cold weather; lastly, goats and sheep, which cost from two to three rupees each, carry from ten to fifteen pounds weight, and do not comparatively suffer from change of climate. The yâks and jooboos are all bred in Bussahir, whence they are brought for sale; and the goats and sheep come from the Chumba district. The feed of these animals costs nothing, they have ample grazing in Thibet, and in the cold weather throughout the whole course of the Aluknunda and Ganges to Nujeebabad, excepting just the day's march about Sreenuggur and Paoree, there is unlimited grazing.

Borax costs, at the mart of Gyanee, from two to three rupees a maund (80 lbs.), it comes from the Chaba lake, which is beyond the Kailas range of hills, about three weeks journey for a drove of goats from Gyanee. At the Lake of Chaba itself, the payment of a tax of one rupee entitles the trader to load his drove with as much borax as they can carry.

The cost of sheep's wool at Daba and Gyanee is one kuldar or Company's rupee for four or five fleeces according to size, it averages one and a half to two annas, or three pence per pound. The cost of pushum varies considerably, and it is generally bought in the goat's fleece mixed with the hair.

The Hunnias are almost entirely dependant on our hill territories for their farinaceous food; the only kind of grain they grow on the table land about the banks of the Sutledge is Oowa, a species of barley, but in small patches only. So sensible are they of their precarious position in this respect, that they keep in stores, throughout Thibet, about three years' supply of grain to provide against any accident interrupting their trade with our territory. As they are thorough barbarians, and their rulers, the Chinese, have a great dread of English travellers or English investigations entering their territories, they might perhaps be starved into relaxing the stringency of their rules against us, by our closing the ghâts, and remitting all dues for the inhabitants of the snow valleys while they were closed; this would, however, injure our own subjects as well as the Hunnias, though the results might be worth temporary inconvenience. There is an enormous amount of raw material of various kinds available in Hundês, and any treaties we may effect at Pekin will not be attended to for years after, if even then, in Thibet.

Our assessment in Kumaon and Gurhwal is very light, more than the revenue being spent in the province by Government for establishments, troops, tea planting, &c., and the traders of the snow valleys who used to pay large sums as taxes to the Ghoorkas, having but little land cultivation, pay us next to nothing. The Commissioners of these districts, which are extra regulation, (*i. e.*, free from the miseries inflicted by our civil courts and their mazes on the people of the plains) have always been very lenient rulers, the Hill men are therefore as loyal as it is possible for Hindoos to be to any Government; they have not yet forgotten the tyranny of the Ghoorkas driven out by General Ochterlony, and have fresh in their recollections the noble exertions of Major Henry Ramsay, C.B., their present commissioner, to relieve their wants during the last two years of famine in the hills.

Judging, therefore, by the accounts of their position which our hill traders give, the Hunnias say that if any foreign raj or government is established in their country, they hope it may not be that of the Sikhs or Ghoorkas, but that they may have the same English raj as our Hill men.

While I was at Kyungrung, the Hunnias were much excited about an expected invasion of the Sikhs from Cashmere viâ Ladakh. They had two years before been attacked by the Ghoorkas, on account of the disputed right to some border villages, and in the time of Runjeet Sing, a large army of Sikhs, under one Jwalla Vizier, invaded their territory. As the Hunnias have no regular troops, and those sent from China take a long time coming, they can make no defence in summer; being, however, a nomade people, when they remove their cattle and families to the mountains, they leave literally nothing for the invader to injure or destroy; their villages are mere encampments of tents, the chief town of Daba has only one stone and mortar built edifice in it, viz., the residence of the Zumpun, while Gartok has two for its officials, all the rest of these cities is composed of woollen and canvas towns of various degrees of dirt. In the winter, however, which is so severe that few invaders of any nation from the southward can live, the Hunnias all return armed as they did on the occasion of Jwalla Vizier's invasion, hang on the flanks of the invading army, cutting off stragglers; and when the Sikhs were dying in hundreds from frost bite, cold and starvation, the Hunnias surrounded and massacred them about Kyungrung and Purung, north of Naipal, where Jwalla Vizier perished with the rest.

I passed several remnants of low stone dikes, while hunting in the nullahs of Salkh and Kyungrung, which had been locations for Hunnias flying from the Sikhs. They told me that the chief part of their defence was entrusted to their Llama, who called down snow in winter to kill their enemies. I pointed out to them that it might be more convenient if, in urgent cases, he would do it in the summer, as I could undertake to perform the former ceremony myself.

My march from Kyungrung by the plains and nullahs around Tazang to Surkya, led me through a country swarming with game. As a spectator stands on the elevated land south of these plains, he sees, to the north, the course of the river Sutledge running from east to west through a table land which is fourteen thousand feet high, and intersected with ravines. The Himalayas, to the south, seem but an ordinary range of hills, scarcely so elevated in appearance as the range beyond the Sutledge, which bounds the view, and in which to the eastward the peak of Kailas rises conspicuous; there are a few groups of small hills here and there on the plains, and large herds of kyang all over them. The kyang are more asinine than equine in appearance, are of a light red colour with white belly and legs, and about fourteen hands high, the hog mane, stripe down the back and tail of the ass, and bray instead of neighing; the head is disproportionately large, and the term, wild horse, a misnomer. There are here and there a few herd of gigantic ovis ammon, the females and young remaining always separate from the males. The horns of the females are remarkably different from those of the males, being but slightly curved, about a foot long and flattish, while the male has a horn like a common English ram, measuring, perhaps, three and a half feet round the curve. Among the hills, at the edge of the plain, are numerous burrul, and the scrub and grass contains a number of large blueish tinted hares, which turn white like the Scotch ones in winter. On the day I marched to Surkya I shot a kyang, several hares, and a hunyâl.

I found the Zumpun waiting for me as promised at Surkya; he had sent two or three messengers to ascertain my progress before I arrived, as he appeared to dread the indignity of having to wait for me, and he sent to inform me, on my arrival, that being on his own side of the ghât, I must visit him at his tent instead of his coming to mine. I therefore walked over to his tent at once, and my advent caused a tremendous routing out of the properties in his, two dirty little canopies, considerable scene shifting inside, being gone through before I was admitted to the august presence. I found the Zumpun a dried up little man of about forty, more Chinese faced than the Hunnias with me, and dressed in a yellow-flowered silk robe, with the usual mandarin hat with red fringe round it, and a plain glass button. He spoke of the capital of the Chinese Empire as "Gyanuk," said he knew the Yang-tse-Kiang river; but had not, so he pretended, heard of the war with the European powers. He ridiculed the report of an invasion of Sikhs, and was very anxious that I should leave as soon as possible. I promised that I would only remain at Surkya for three days, but refused his request that I should go back through the Niti ghât, as I was determined to kill a bunchowr, if practicable, in the Keo nullahs or Leptel.

The Zumpun had brought a Llama with him, as a sort of domestic chaplain, who had

J. Wolf, del.

M & N Hanhart lith.

HEEMACHUL AND ITS INHABITANTS.

his hair cropt short, and wore a dull red coloured robe after the manner of his kind. I thought him wonderfully like a Jesuit, a high forehead, hollow cheeks, aquiline nose, instead of the usual Hunnia snub, a sensual mouth, and a sinister leer in the eyes—altogether very good raw material for the make up of a fashionable Puseyite father confessor. The Zumpun having about a dozen attendants and his little son with him, I took my Shikaree Kunhaya and two of my Bompa men as interpreters to the audience. Some of the usual thick soupy Hunnia tea was presented to me, and I managed two mouthfuls without being sick, but was obliged to declare that, even at the risk of eternal war between our nations, I must protest against drinking any more of that medicine. I offered to make some, English fashion, for the Zumpun; but he declined with a request that I should send him the dry tea instead. I presented a dozen stereocopic pictures to "Zumpun fils;" they were examined upside down, lengthways, crossways, and rubbed with dirty fingers to see if any "development" could thereby be produced, and were finally pronounced to be "nothing;" but the first of these seen in the stereoscope caused a scream of delight, and the Zumpun had to take snuff continuously, which he supplied himself with from a green agate bottle, like a scent bottle, in order to keep his intellects up to the mark in examining such wonders.

I gave the old gentleman a bottle of essence of rose as a substitute for his snuff, but it was declared by all the Hunnias, who smelt it in turn, to be very nasty. The English ladies depicted on the stereoscopic slides, were considered decidedly inferior in beauty to the hippopotamus-faced Houris of Hundês, but the photograph being now at Daba, may in time improve their taste. On parting with the Zumpun, he told me that he should be obliged to leave next day, as the smell of the kyang which I had shot, and which was about two miles off, made him faint. He must have had considerable inventive genius to think of this fable, for all the dead horses in

China, would not within five hours, taint the air like one live Hunnia. He presented me with a specimen of Daba woollen manufacture, a couple of yâk tails, and a cap of very fine felt, which might have fitted my head at six months old, but looked like a tea cup on it when presented—we parted of course sworn friends.

I next day killed four kyang, a hunyal, and so many hares, that all my camp was supplied with hare soup. The day after I secured a fine ovis ammon, and the next managed to shoot a kyang mare of which I caught the foal; this I picketted in front of my tent, but as it disappeared during the night, though too young to wander far, or forage for itself, I suspect the Hunnias must have appropriated it. I was very anxious to push on to the Chaba Lake, on hearing from my men that no European had visited it; but the Hunnias declared they had orders to fight, if I marched further into their territory. My promise to the Zumpun rendered it impossible for me to remain longer without his leave, and I dreaded coming to blows with the Hunnias, as though they were comparatively harmless, it would compromise me with my own Government.

I left the Tazang plains with regret, and in three days entered the Keo nullahs.

The Hunnia guard who still watched me closely, informed me that I had no chance of finding bunchowr that year, as the bulls only came once in winter to our hills, and always returned to visit their families on the Gangri hills by Gartok in the beginning of July. I nevertheless determined to use every precaution in approaching the last locality, where I could hope for the game I had come so far to obtain. I would not permit the camp to ascend far up the nullah, and directed my men to pitch low down, close by the principal stream, in as sheltered a spot as they could find.

I went over a good deal of ground the first day of my arrival, and found fresh traces, but saw no bunchowr; burrul were numerous, but not worth shooting, at the risk of scaring nobler game. On the second day I was to conclude my search, but sufficient ground remained unvisited in the Keo nullahs to occupy one long day's march; and although Dhun Sing had all along declared that the big bull of Salkh nullah must have gone to Keo, I set off to climb the heights commanding the furthest course of the stream with sundry misgivings as to the result. We traversed some eight or ten miles of ground without seeing anything, when the quick eye of my guide, Buchoo, detected a black spot a long way off, which a careful inspection with my binocular glass proved to be a bunchowr; we had been west, north, and east of the spot without being within sight, and having, fortunately, a southern breeze, he lay chewing the cud in sublime indifference as to our neighbourhood. There was, however, no cover to stalk him by, except on the south side, but as we should have only a hundred and fifty yards to go after he had winded us, I determined on risking it, making straight for a stone about seventy yards from him, without daring to look up till we reached it, then found that the bull had scented us and risen to make off; but it was too late, the bunchowr never moves far when wounded, apparently stupified by its effect, though he sometimes charges fiercely at the hunter if he shows himself. A ball from my rifle in the shoulder, and another in the haunch which lamed him, sealed his fate, he only moved a short distance, while we followed up, and when he turned round to look at us; my two attendants commenced shouting, on which he shook his horns and brought down his head to charge on three legs, but a ball in the shoulder, laming another leg, rendered charging impossible, and two more shots at close quarters finished him. The legs are so short that his sinking on his chest did not much reduce his height, he had an unusual amount of long hair all along the flanks and legs, though the back was smooth; he measured nine feet round the chest, while his horns were sixteen inches in circumference at the base, and eleven inches half way up. He appeared full front like an enormous American bison, and would, I believe, weigh considerably more than that animal, though not so high at the wither from the shortness of his legs, which, being almost lost in the long hair of his flanks, gave him a petticoated appearance.

As the day was closing when bunchowr died, we made at once for our tents, carrying off the tail as a proof of our success, and I found it equal in size and weight to three of the tame yâk tails which I had purchased. Two days were devoted by myself and men to removing the skin, and preparing the head for transport. The Hunnias not only assisted in the work, but feasted with great delight on the flesh, which I found to be excellent beef. Many of the men, being Rajpoots, could not, of course, eat the flesh of an animal, bearing so much resemblance to the sacred Brahminee Bull; and their activity in hunting, and all except actually eating him, proves how far Hindoos will forget their prejudices unless continually recalled to their recollection by the nervousness or indiscretion of Englishmen; some of whom are more bigotted in favour of Hindoo whimsies, and high or low caste distinctions, than the Hindoos themselves, who most naturally take a "religious prejudice" against everything they dislike, or don't choose to do, if they find that such a course frightens both private individuals and government into submission to their wishes, but who forget their oldest antipathies if properly managed.

The best method of preserving and preparing skins, is that adopted by the American Indians for their buffalo robes, being nothing but careful and minute removal of all flesh or fat from the hide, and continued rubbing with rounded pieces of bone or wood, till the permanent softening of the skin is effected. As this takes some days to accomplish, and it is necessary to keep the skin moist all the time, it should be rolled up carefully when the day's work is over and put into a wet cloth for the night. This plan of preparing skins is of course impossible in the plains, where the heat causes decomposition within twenty-four hours: I used, therefore, simply to stretch out the skin on the ground by small wooden pegs driven into the edge of it, and leave it to dry in the sun, which took three or four hours, or else sprinkle the inside with wood ashes, or a little lime water; this latter plan is always objected to by the dressers who have to prepare the skin afterwards, on the ground that it burns them, and makes softening sometimes impossible.

Four days later our party arrived at Rimkim, for the second transit of the Chor Hoti, and, starting at daylight, found the state of the snow and weather so favourable, that we arrived by noon at Kala Jubbur. The men were in high spirits, and proposed pushing on at once for Bompa, running three marches into one, which they easily effected on my promising them, if they did it, three days pay for the work.

Though familiar with many strange scenes in the hunting ground of the snows, the most ordinary sights of an inhabited quarter had, even after so short an absence, all the freshness of novelty, and on approaching our villages one of the young Coolees raised a laugh by pointing in an excited manner, as if sighting a wild yâk, to a speck near the village of Niti, and gravely announcing "Wuh to Zenani hai!" "That is a woman!"

Our arrival, and the motley display of skins, horns, and tails, produced great excitement among the dirty looking denizens of Bompa, where my men devoted two days to feasting, while I packed my traps for Mussouree. Having nothing further to gain in the hunting line near Bompa, I would not wait for fine weather, but made up my mind to face a fortnight's march through the rain.

My deductions from my labours through the Mountains of Hundês being—the discovery frequently made by sportsmen, and, perhaps, fully equal to what has already been produced by "mountains in labour"—that if I could only have started with all the experience with which I returned, my bag must have been infinitely heavier!

In conclusion, I beg to offer a word of parting advice to my brother sportsmen, on a subject more important than venerie. I regret to say I have known many cases where Englishmen, once removed from home scenes and associations, and among a heathen people, deem the due observance of Christian sabbaths no longer imperative, and falsely fancying that their Mahommedan or idolatrous associates will ascribe to liberality of feeling a forgetfulness or indifference to the forms of their faith, hunt and shoot indiscriminately on every day of the week. I believe that such a course not only does not increase the attachment, but materially lessens the respect of their native subordinates.

I know there are men who, on the highest principles, will jealously cherish that attachment and respect for our Christian sabbaths, which they imbibed in English homes with the earliest germs of manly English feeling; but even, if no better motive existed, I feel assured that on every consideration, even of expediency and good policy, it is desirable to hold at least one day for rest and reflection, when the English hunter in the farthest gorges of the Himalaya, or the wildest plains of Thibet, perhaps sole representative of his nation, may for a space forget foreign influences—the dusky forms or the mighty snow peaks around him—to picture scenes in a dearer country, and though far from the reach of church bells reflect

"How many happy groups this day are bending,
Through England's primrose meadow paths, their way
Towards spire and tower, 'midst shadowy elms ascending,
Whence the sweet chimes proclaim the hallowed day;
The halls from old heroic ages gray,
Pour their fair children forth, and hamlets low,
With whose thick orchard-blooms the soft winds play,
Send out their inmates in a happy flow."

CHAPTER XII.

RIFLES AND GUNS.

Smooth-bore.—Breech-loading.—Measurement for stock.—Bakers and Galton's opinions on guage and sighting.—Metford's shells.—Challenge cup rifle match at Dehra.—Best kind of Rifle barrels.—Whitworth's improvements.—Details to be defined in ordering a rifle or gun.

I HAVE experimentalized with almost every kind of rifle and gun, and think the simplest plan for imparting experience on the subject, will be to describe merely the weapons which I believe the best for all purposes, and the principle reasons for my conclusions, without attempting to detail the peculiarities of weapons I could not recommend.

As regards the smooth bore, there is no doubt, I believe, but that ere long breech-loaders will supersede all others; their advantages are manifest and numerous, while their present disadvantages are attributable to mechanical deficiencies, which in course of time will doubtless be removed. I believe the best breech-loader at present known, is Messrs. Callisher and Terry's, not only because of its strength and simplicity, but because the gun can be used with ordinary ammunition as a muzzle loader. This is, of course, a great advantage for Indian use, because until breech-loaders are much more common than they are at present, cartridges may at times be unprocurable; and in heavy game shooting, moreover, it is often desirable to add, when loading, two or three drams more than the ordinary charge of powder. The cartridge, however, for Terry's patent can be made by the sportsman himself, being cased in thin paper only, in lieu of the common copper capsule. The best guage for general shooting, and especially Himalayan shooting is fourteen, it is large enough for any

It is absolutely necessary for hill pheasant shooting, that the sportsman possess a gun that will kill at unusually long distances. It is always better to have too much than too little power in a gun, indeed you can hardly have one too powerful, as a little extra weight is of no consequence when your gun is almost always carried for you. I know, by long experience, that alignment is much surer with a long gun than a short one; and, also, that although nothing is more common than for careless talkers to boast of some particular short barrel of their own, which throws or rather is said to throw closer than any long gun, and to generalize on the supposed fact—as a rule, no short gun can compete with a longer one of equally efficient and careful workmanship.

I should therefore recommend a sportsman of average stature and strength, to have his gun not less than thirty-four inches in barrel, and if of superior height and more than average strength, he should have it thirty-six inches; the shape and length of the stock should of course depend on the shape and make of the owner's arms, shoulders and neck. A stock should be made to measure, instead of a sportsman trying to twist his own figure and mode of shooting to a shape which he has purchased, without any reference to his own figure.

A straightish stock has many advantages in lessening the effects of displacement caused by recoil; a very crooked stock, if the gun kicks at all, must throw up the barrels and necessarily hurt the cheek, as the shoulder is out of the line of recoil. I myself like what is called a long straightish stock with a pistol-handled grip.

The annexed diagram will show the system adopted by the trade to measure the bend of a stock, and will enable any one in India who has a favourite and suitable stock to take its measure, and get one like it without sending it home to be copied.

A straight rod of wood C D being laid on the barrels, the length of the dotted line A gives the bend of the stock at the cheek, that at B the bend at the heel. The length of the stock is the distance E F from the first trigger to the bend of the heel plate.

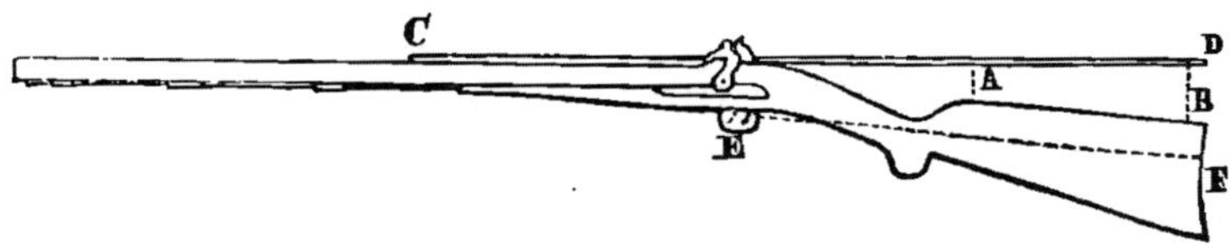

There are some valuable hints contained in the opinions recorded as to guage and sighting in Messrs. Baker's and Galton's works. I have tested in practise the truth of the general principles they enunciate, and give their opinions in their own words. Baker says, page 135, of "The Rifle and the Hound in Ceylon :"

"With these elephants, the four ounce rifle (No. 4 guage) is an invaluable weapon; even if the animal is not struck on the mortal spot, the force of the blow upon his head is so great that it will generally bring him upon his knees or at least stop him. It has failed once or twice in this, but not often; and on those occasions I had loaded with the conical ball. This, although it will penetrate much farther through a thick substance than a round ball, is not so effective in elephant shooting as the latter. The reason is plain enough. No shot in the head will kill an elephant dead, unless it passes through the brain; an ounce ball will effect this as well as a six pound shot; but there are many cases where the brain cannot be touched, by a peculiar method of carrying the head and trunk in charging &c., a power is then required, that by the concussion will knock him down.

" The four ounce conical ball should be an excellent weapon for African shooting, when the usual shot at an elephant is at the shoulder. This shot would never answer in Ceylon: the country is not sufficiently open to watch the effects produced upon the animals, and although he may have a mortal wound, he carries it away with him, and is not bagged. I have frequently tried this shot; and, although I have seen the elephants go away with ears and trunk drooping, still

I have never bagged more than one by any but the head shot."

It must be remembered that this four ounce carrying rifle, though only a single barrel, weighed 21 lbs. and even at that weight recoiled unpleasantly. I recommend the shells which have since been perfected, as giving the shock to the system which can render one shot instantaneously fatal or paralyzing, though not in brain, heart, or spine, though fired from a 12 or 15lb. double rifle, of only the Government twenty-four guage, with a proportionately heavy charge of powder, but with absolute immobility as to recoil or ringing of the barrel.

Where shells, from their expence or any other cause are not intended to be used, the principle pointed out in the above quotation should be attended to. It was frequently found during the Indian mutiny, that Colt's revolver (navy size) though the best of all in other respects, had so small and so sharply pointed a bullet, that there was but little immediate paralysing effect when it was fired into the body of a man; and that an opponent, so wounded, could after it cut you down with a sword, or bayonet you, though the pistol wound proved ultimately mortal on himself. The calibre of our present army guns and rifles has been reduced to twenty-four, and it is in contemplation to reduce them considerably more; this will, I fancy, be carried to an extreme. Sharpshooters may be more efficient, and attain to greater accuracy, by retaining the full weight of the rifle, but reducing to a limited extent its calibre; but the fire of the line at close quarters must be less effective, and flesh wounds by little picket bullets are almost always trifling.

Francis Galton in his "Art of Travel," page 137, says very truly. "American bushrangers advocate a long heavy pea rifle, on the plea of its accurate shooting, and the enormous saving in weight gained by using bullets of a small size. The only objections to small bored rifles are those of insufficiency against very large game, even when conical bullets are used, and a tendency to become foul after a very few shots. A short light rifle, whether with large or small bores, is, I believe, utterly worthless.

"In the hands of a man trembling with running, or with exhaustion, it shakes like a wand; and the shorter the rifle, the more quickly does it oscillate, and in the very same proportion is it more difficult to catch the exact moment when the sights cover the object.

"In all cases, the hind sight should be far from the eye, even halfway down the barrel, else it becomes quite out of focus and indistinct, when the eye is firmly set on the object aimed at, and this drawback much more than compensates for any advantage that is gained by having the front and hind sights far asunder."

I think that this principle of long barrels admits of some modification—thus for intance a 15lb rifle, if of considerable length, would from its leverage feel very much heavier; in fact be, in effective result on the arm, much heavier than a 15lb rifle of only twenty-four inches in the barrel, the latter may be used with facility by many persons who could not support the other steadily. I have, however, frequently tested the truth of the observation as to the advisability of focussing the sights, and it is a point on which, because "unusual in the trade," rifle makers are often obstinate.

I have noted "two hundred copper tubes for Jacob's shells," as an item in the list of articles to be taken out from England, by any sportsman bent on doing execution among the game of the Himalaya or elsewhere. These tubes cannot be got or imitated effectively in India, and are very expensive even in England. It is convenient, under any circumstances, to have a small supply at hand; but the courtesy of Captain Warlow R.A., the Government Inspector of small arms at Birmingham, enables me to present to my readers an invention at once cheap, simple, and effective, which appears to me to combine all that is wanted in rifle shells for sporting purposes. It is the invention of a young civil engineer of the name of Metford, who, finding that the Jacob shell did not at times explode on coming in contact with the flesh of an animal, adopted, as his explosive agent, a mixture of equal parts of chlorate of potass and sulphate of antimony. The two can be mixed together on a plate with a bone paper cutter or a pen, the more they are mixed, the more sensitive their detonating power becomes. The bullets are moulded with a hole from the apex to about one third from the base, just as for Jacob's shells, but no copper tubes are used, the powder is filled in with a quill to the top, then settled down by a few taps of the base of the bullet on a table, and the space left at the top filled up with bees' wax, thus:

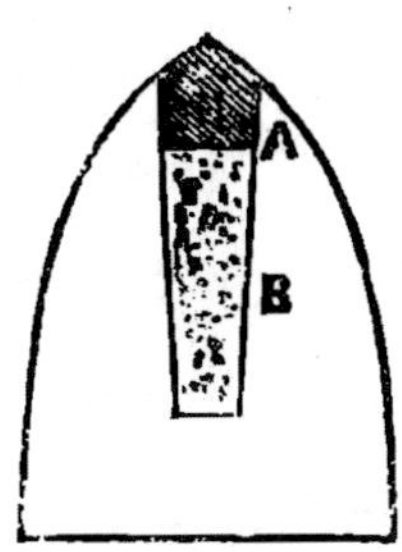

These shells will not only explode on

striking an animal, but ignite on being fired into water. The important difference in the result of a day's shooting in the Doon, which the use of such missiles must insure, may be guessed at from the instances I have already mentioned, of ninety bullets being sometimes fired to only five animals bagged, some twenty additional ones must have been wounded under such circumstances, but the use of Metford's shells, though but slightly increasing the cost of ammunition, must insure almost every animal hit being secured.

Rifle shooting is a common amusement at all our Hill stations, gentlemen there, being almost all "on leave," have plenty of time for practising, and rifles, as a matter of course, are brought in great numbers to a game district. Major Skinner, a son of the famous Colonel Skinner of the Hurrianah Irregular Horse, who rose to fame in the chivalrous age of our Anglo-Indian history, used to promote rifle practice and competition by his public spirited hospitality to all lovers of the art. Frequent meetings to contest for prizes, with varying results, at his residence, led to some general matches at Dehra, and ultimately to a match in 1855 for a plate, value £100, made by Hunt and Roskell. Thirty competitors appeared for this match, and the results of the shooting will probably convince most English riflemen that, at present, they would find themselves more than a match for the majority of Indian sportsmen.

The distances at which competition took place, were those most useful for sporting purposes: viz., one hundred, one hundred and fifty, two hundred, and two hundred and fifty yards. Three shots being fired by each competitor at each of these distances, and the aggregate of the distances of all the shots from the pin's-point in the centre, regulated the marksman's position in the final list, the shortest string, of course, winning. The target was an iron hoop, with a diameter of six feet, covered with cloth and white paper, the only black mark being a bull's-eye of six inches diameter. All black circles or rings are objectionable as they detract from the clearness of the bull's-eye.

Many of the members having implicit confidence in the experience of English riflemakers, perseveringly continued practising for the match with the old polygroove sporting rifles of heavy calibre and comparatively light weight, there were even three rifles of this style expressly commissioned for the match, from Messrs. Smith, of Princes Street, Leicester Square, the cost of a single barrel being 400 rupees, or £40. As I was, even then, fully aware that impenetrable obstinacy to any kind of improvement had thrown our makers far behind the Americans and Swiss, I got possession of a 60 dollar, £6 rifle, by Edwin Wesson, of Massachusetts, a long heavy barrel, increasing twist, picket ball, polygroove, and very finely sighted. The performances of this weapon were so superior to the slovenly Minie principle English weapons, or the antiquated old English, or mediæval polygroove and round ball, that my competitors, though they ridiculed my bad taste and want of judgment in the choice of a weapon, soon found that they had no chance at all in the match. My first shot at two hundred and fifty yards was eighteen inches from the pin's-point, but all the rest, eleven in number, were within a radius of twelve inches; this, though steady, was not good shooting, yet it won the cup by "a long chalk," the plunging round-shot of the sporting poly-groove being "nowhere." This country owes much to General John Jacob, and Mr. Whitworth, the great improvers of the English rifle.

Very great improvements have, as all know, been effected in English rifles, since a period just prior to the Crimean war, and a complete revolution has been effected in the enterprize and capabilities of our rifle manufacturers. Up to that time they were generally so wedded to their own routine system of manufacture, so self-sufficient as to what rifle users ought to want, and so indifferent as to what improvers actually wanted, that their weapons were objects of ridicule and contempt at all the great American and Swiss matches. At present, although great improvements have been effected in army rifles, we are still far from perfect as regards weapons for sporting purposes.

The best barrelling, indeed the only one I consider which in point of finished accuracy is fit for a sportsman's weapon, is that on the mechanical adaptation principle, in which the bullet is shaped exactly or mechanically to fit the interior, or the lands and creeses as they are technically called, of the barrel.

General Jacob's and Whitworth's rifles are different specimens of this principle, but neither Mr. Whitworth, or Messrs. Witton and Daw, who principally manufacture the Jacob rifle, have yet perfected any breech-loading for them, and Messrs. Callisher and Terry, as yet, apply their patent to the Minie principle barrels only, in which the sides of the projectile are a smooth cone, and are blown into the grooving, or expanded to fit the shape of the bore by the explosive force of the powder, or else by a small box-wood peg being driven by the explosion into the hollow of the projectile.

The Minie system was of course of very great service in the army, when muzzle loading only was known, as great facility for loading was combined with great propelling power; but, as regards accuracy of fire, it is a very clumsy contrivance; but accuracy, great force, and facility of loading would all be combined, if the combination of the breech-loader and the mechanically adapted conical ball plan was effected.

The advantage of using the Government Enfield ammunition with the new breech-loader, will doubtless perpetuate for some time the Minie principle, but it will be driven out of the field if Mr. Whitworth can perfect his weapon, by applying an efficient loading breech to it.

The Lancaster rifle is the most accurate Government weapon used at present. It has at any rate often beaten the Enfield; Jacob's rifle is very much superior to either of them, while Whitworth's is the best of all, though its superiority to the Jacob is chiefly due, I believe, to its extreme accuracy of manufacture.

Jacob's shells can be used with either Whitworth's or Jacob's rifles, and in a suitable breech-loader their use would be rendered perfectly safe.

I consider that the two most novel facts enunciated by Mr. Whitworth during his late experiments with rifled cannon at Southport are, firstly. That the reduction of the diameter of the base of his projectile increased its flight at long ranges by five hundred yards.

Every one would naturally suppose that the base of a conical projectile should exactly fill the bore of its weapon, and that the surface to be acted on by the projecting power would thus be better adapted to operate on; but Mr. Whitworth found that something like the run or lines of a steamer through the water, adopting a beam, or widest diameter for the projectile, at which point he mechanically fits it to his hexagon bore, and tapering it off both fore and aft improves its flight.

The cause has not been clearly determined, but it appears to be principally attributable to the reduction of the area of vacuity which the rapid flight of the projectile causes behind, and which is equal to 15lbs. on two square inches.

The next important fact, is the effect produced in penetrating iron sheeting, or passing through water when the point of the projectile is cut square off; pointed or round-headed projectiles have a tendency to tear and rend iron sheeting, while Whitworth's square cut iron bolt punches out a hole with a clean cut. The tendency of a ball, whether round or conical, to glance from the surface of water is well known, and the difficulty consequently found in fish shooting, unless the fish come to the surface; but one of Whitworth's flat-headed heavy shot "has made its way through twenty-seven feet of water, and then penetrated a thick wooden butt."

I annex a note of the details which should be defined when ordering a gun or rifle, the measurement are those which I adopt, but may, of course, be easily altered to suit the person ordering them.

1st. A double gun, breech-loading, (maker?) 14 bore, 36 barrels, length of stock $14\frac{1}{2}$ inches, bend at cheek $1\frac{3}{8}$ inch, at heel plate $1\frac{3}{4}$ inch, pistol handled grip, entire weight 9lbs.

In case with fittings complete.

As perfect a weapon, in all essentials, as can be made in England is worth £25.

2nd. A double rifle, Jacob's grooving and twist, regulation bore, hexagon shaped barrels outside, length of barrels 24 inches, fly sight beaded and very fine, a block back sight which with fly is parrellel to bore, *folding* sights for hundred and two hundred yards, spring sight to two thousand yards, the sights to be fixed half way up the barrel, *i. e.*, 12 inches from muzzle, and graduated for the position, hair triggers, in case with fittings complete.

As perfect a weapon, in all essentials, as can be made in England is worth thirty guineas.

THE END.